Praise for
Homegrown Democrat

"A graceful, loving celebration of the old-time Minnesota liberalism of the heart that is so sorely missed in today's politics."
—*The Washington Post*

"Heartfelt . . . Practically glows with goodwill and good feeling."
—*The Boston Globe*

"Peerless . . . still makes me laugh every time I read it, which is often."
—Katharine Powers, *The Boston Globe*

"[S]incere, and fervid, and funny, and outrageous . . . [*Homegrown Democrat*] offers passion, and then some. . . If you're a Democrat, read it and get aroused."
—*St. Louis Post-Dispatch*

"[A]t once tendentious, fed-up, and funny."
—*Star Tribune* (Minneapolis)

"Let's start the campaign today: Keillor in 2008."
—*The Christian Science Monitor*

"[A book] of grace, empathy, and insight."
—*The American Prospect*

"It teaches with humor and without most of the bile."
—*The Roanoke Times and World News*

"[A]ll will appreciate Keillor's candor in distancing core Roo-seveltian values from certain tendencies of political correctness and Yuppie hubris." —*Library Journal*

"A heartwarming case for liberalism." —*Publishers Weekly*

PENGUIN BOOKS
HOMEGROWN DEMOCRAT

GARRISON KEILLOR is the host and writer of *A Prairie Home Companion*, the author of sixteen books, including the Lake Wobegon novels and *Daddy's Girl*, and the editor of *Good Poems* and *Good Poems for Hard Times*. His syndicated column, "The Old Scout," is seen in papers coast to coast. A member of the Academy of American Arts and Letters, he lives in St. Paul, Minnesota.

HOMEGROWN DEMOCRAT

A Few Plain Thoughts from the Heart of America

REVISED AND UPDATED

GARRISON KEILLOR

* * *

*

PENGUIN BOOKS

PENGUIN BOOKS

Published by the Penguin Group

Penguin Group (USA) Inc., 375 Hudson Street, New York, New York 10014, U.S.A.
Penguin Group (Canada), 90 Eglinton Avenue East, Suite 700, Toronto, Ontario,
Canada M4P 2Y3 (a division of Pearson Penguin Canada Inc.)
Penguin Books Ltd, 80 Strand, London WC2R 0RL, England
Penguin Ireland, 25 St Stephen's Green, Dublin 2, Ireland
(a division of Penguin Books Ltd)
Penguin Group (Australia), 250 Camberwell Road, Camberwell, Victoria 3124,
Australia (a division of Pearson Australia Group Pty Ltd)
Penguin Books India Pvt Ltd, 11 Community Centre, Panchsheel Park,
New Delhi – 110 017, India
Penguin Group (NZ), cnr Airborne and Rosedale Roads, Albany, Auckland 1310,
New Zealand (a division of Pearson New Zealand Ltd)
Penguin Books (South Africa) (Pty) Ltd, 24 Sturdee Avenue, Rosebank,
Johannesburg 2196, South Africa

Penguin Books Ltd, Registered Offices:
80 Strand, London WC2R 0RL, England

First published in the United States of America by Viking Penguin, a member of
Penguin Group (USA) Inc. 2004
This revised and updated edition published in Penguin Books 2006

10 9 8 7 6 5 4 3 2 1

THE LIBRARY OF CONGRESS HAS CATALOGED THE HARDCOVER EDITION AS FOLLOWS:
Keillor, Garrison.
Homegrown democrat / Garrison, Keillor.
p. cm.
ISBN 0-670-03365-0 (hc.)
ISBN 0 14 30.3768 4 (pbk.)
1. Democracy—United States.   2. United States—Politics and government.
3. Keillor, Garrison.   4. Authors, American—20th century—Biography.   5. Radio
broadcasters—United States—Biography.   6. Democratic Party (U.S.)
7. Republican Party (U.S.: 1854–ソ)   8. United States—Economic policy.
9. United States—Social policy.   10. Minnesota—Social conditions.   I. Title.
JK1726.K37 2004
320.973—dc22   2004053565

Printed in the United States of America
Set in Aldus
Designed by Carla Bolte

TO THE MEN AND WOMEN ACROSS
OUR COUNTRY
WHO ONE DAY DECIDED THAT, DESPITE ALL
SENSIBLE REASONS NOT TO DO IT,
THEY WOULD, IN GOOD FAITH,
OUT OF GRATITUDE,
RUN FOR PUBLIC OFFICE

✳✳✳✳ CONTENTS ✳✳✳✳

DON'T
THINK ILL
of
DEMOCRATS,
YOU MAY BE
ONE OF US.

* * *
*

IT'S A GREAT country. I went to the *Paris Review* gala at Cipriani's in New York and during the after-dinner speeches I moseyed off to the men's room and there, amid marble splendor, stood Carl Bernstein at the urinal, the journalist who Dustin Hoffman played in *All the President's Men*. I stationed myself a few feet away and then heard a haranguing voice from the corner. The old black washroom attendant was telling Bernstein what a great man Richard Nixon was and how a bunch of third-raters like Bernstein had brought him down. The journalist gave me a wan smile. "I keep running into him," he said. The old man was really pissed. "He was one of the greatest presidents this country ever had and he was vilified for what? For diddly-squat!" Mr. Bernstein washed his hands. The old man handed him a towel: "You ought to be ashamed of yourself," he said. Mr. Bernstein put a dollar in the tip jar and slipped away. "You a friend of his?" the old man said. "Me? I'm from Minnesota." A great democratic country. LOWER-ECHELON SERVICE EMPLOYEE HARASSES FAMOUS WRITER IN PISSOIR.

Once I got on the subway at 96th and Broadway, heading downtown, I noticed that the woman sitting opposite me was reading my *Book of Guys*. She was black, well dressed, thirtyish, close-cropped hair, and she sat reading the book, expressionless, past 86th, 79th, 72nd, 66th, 59th, and 50th. She didn't laugh or even smile, but she didn't snap the book shut and roll her eyes either. She kept reading. The train rattled downtown past Times Square and Penn Station and finally at 14th Street I had to get off. The tension was too much. The author was starting to feel as if her disdain might break his heart, and he climbed the stairs to 7th Avenue and got in a cab. The pure democracy of literature:

one author, one reader. We can't get away from each other.

I live in St. Paul, Minnesota, where the crab apple tree beside our house is putting on a show of purple petals that suggests a float in the Mardi Gras parade, and for a Minnesota stoic it's quite a sight. You can almost hear saxophones playing "Moon River." Purple petals collect on the windshield of my car, down in the recess where the wipers live, and when I drive down the street, purple petals fly out, a flurry of them, such as might signal a flashback in a movie. I drive to work and walk down the hall to my office, which is small, cluttered, piles of books, unanswered mail, and a couple of grandsons smiling out from a picture frame. And a picture of Paul and Sheila Wellstone. I was sitting in this chair in October 2002, when I heard that their plane had crashed up north. No survivors.

I disagreed with Paul about many things, but when the people of Minnesota, after Paul's death, voted for an empty suit, a glib, soulless man, it felt like your father running away with Amber the 18-year-old cocktail waitress with blue hair. Poor deluded man. What was he drinking?

I was in San Francisco the morning after Election Day, in exquisite pain, and had a cup of coffee with the poet Lawrence Ferlinghetti, whom I had never met before, at the Caffé Greco on Columbus Avenue in North Beach near the old "marzipan church" that he has written about, and Washington Square with the park benches and old Italians "with gnarled hands and wild eyebrows / the ones with the baggy pants with both belt & suspenders / the grappa drinkers with teeth like corn." Ferlinghetti was a handsome figure at 83, in a red shirt and jeans and running shoes, white hair and the trim beard of a boulevardier. His father came to New York City from Italy in 1896, an auctioneer and minor mafioso, and Ferlinghetti, having taken part in D-Day and attended the Sorbonne on the G.I. Bill, painting and translating poetry, landed in San Francisco in 1950 with a duffel bag over his shoulder. "I liked the city," he said. "It had this insular feeling, like Naples. People there are Neapolitans first and Italians second. I came to North Beach, which was 90% Italian then, and here I am."

I love his poem about an Italian funeral at the Green Street Mortuary—"That's just around the corner," he said—and the gallant marching band that precedes the hearse, playing a stirring march "as if it were celebrating life and never heard of death with the trombones and the tuba and the trumpets and the big bass drum and the corpse hears nothing or everything and it's a glorious autumn day in old North Beach if only he could have lived to see it only we wouldn't have had the band." A Midwesterner hikes around San Francisco and along the Marina among the Frisbee-chasing dogs and kite flyers and feels the pull—a seaport town is more tolerant of human nature—it encouraged Mark Twain and Allen Ginsberg both—he looks at the boats sailing out through the Golden Gate and he looks at Fort Mason, once a major embarkation point for troops going to Vietnam, now home to crafts shops and fine restaurants, and he can hear the big bass drum booming—things change, that's how we know we're alive—and he looks forward to the next chapter of the story, hoping the parade will turn the corner and not march off the end of the wharf.

Politics is transitory. The new names go up on the marquee, the old ones come down. The young raccoons challenge the old, there's some shrieking and screeching, and the old ones slink away. Newt is king of the hill for a day or two, and then he's just one more large white man eating creamed chicken at the Rotary lunch.

The big huffers and woofers of the Republican Revolution in Washington have gone the way of all flesh. They took over Congress and the White House, horns blew, church bells rang, people ran into the streets, sailors kissed each other, and what happened? They led us into a reckless foreign war and brought death and suffering to people they don't care about and squandered the good name of America and steered the economy toward receivership by cutting taxes and growing government and they wielded power as if there were no rules. They openly, brazenly, countenanced crimes of torture at Guantánamo, Abu Ghraib and Bagram. They engaged in illegal surveillance and they arrested people without charge and "disappeared" them to foreign jails. Meanwhile, the money flowed from the lobbyists to the campaign coffers to the congressional nest eggs and government expanded as Republican cronies and nephews and sons-in-law found well-paid positions: Republicans believe in deregulation, but it takes more and more of them to not regulate us. And now, having gone about as far as they can go, they are bankrupt.

They have played the terrorism card for all it is worth, have campaigned successfully against flag-burners and baby-killers and secular humanists and Adam and Steve, have fleeced whole flocks of Christians, but they are done for, kaput, for one reason. They don't represent the country. If they ever did, they don't anymore.

And the Chief Occupant—what is one to make of him? This is a man who should not have sought public office. A man with almost nothing admirable in his résumé. He has been cruelly exposed as incompetent, inarticulate, and dishonest. His inattention is remarkable. He sat and was briefed on the danger of a hurricane wiping out a major American city, and without asking a single question, he got up from the table and walked away and resumed his monthlong vacation. He played guitar as New Orleans was flooded. It took him four days to realize he ought to pay attention. When the tsunami killed a hundred thousand people in southeast Asia, he was on vacation and it took him seventy-two hours to issue a statement of sympathy. A small petulant man who keeps diminishing with time—the headline of an AP story, BUSH URGES CONFIDENCE IN HIS LEADERSHIP, says so much—until even those who once ticked the lever beside his name look at him in disbelief. How did this man come to represent our country?

It's true, what our parents told us: it only takes one person to mess things up for everybody.

That gumball Richard Reid, on a Paris-to-Miami flight, tried to set fire to his explosive shoes and thanks to him we airline passengers must take off our shoes at the security checkpoint and waltz through the metal detector in stocking feet, a testimony to Mr. Reid's enduring influence. Someday, someone will try to scoot through with an underwear bomb and then we'll have to arrive at the airport three hours early and wait in line to be inspected by specially trained crotch-sniffing dogs.

And George W. Bush, single-handedly exercising his power of inattention, has brought this country to a perilous point, spending blood and treasure on a crusade to push ever deeper into the swamp, to the despair of a growing majority of Americans. It isn't much of a mystery. He's a man who is intellectually and temperamentally unequipped to rise to the challenges of his office. He's a rigid and incurious man overwhelmed by events in a world in which he is isolated and can't look around and see. He is a turtle on a fence post.

*

America at its best is a generous and redemptive land occupied by amiable, optimistic, sentimental, humorous people. Europeans can be shocked at how reflexively friendly we can be with people we don't know. We meet strangers over a cup of coffee and suddenly we're telling about the crazy uncle who ran off with the church secretary. We rally to help people we never met. Amiability is the basis of civil politics: you don't cheat people you like; you don't abuse people who might become your friends.

That's the America I know, the nation of Kiwanians and Mennonites and generous teachers and parents. It's out there, even if you can't find it on the radio anymore. It survives the angry Visigoths on the freeway and the inhuman office parks and the greasy politicians harrumphing about values. The old amiable America lives on. I find it at state fairs where people come to view pigs the size of Volkswagens and eat deep-fried broccoli and ride inside something like a salad spinner and look at threshing machines and dangerous pythons and blue-ribbon pies and bushels of apples. You bite into an apple at the fair and it's even better than the apples of your youth. A generation of horticulturism has given us ever finer apples, and from the apple, and from the apple-based pie, one can take courage. The old amiable America can reassert itself. Yes, the country has been badly dented in the past twelve years. There is more information technology and less interest in facts, more communication, less comprehension. Fewer journalists and more vice presidents for organizational resource imaging. This is troubling. But don't lose hope.

The government of our good country has been heisted by cynics and crooks, and their chutzpah is astonishing. If your alderman introduced a resolution in the city council called the Salute to Our Boys in Uniform Resolution, which, in small print in section II, division A, paragraph 4, line 122, includes a provision giving his brother-in-law Walt the contract to haul garbage, the Honorable would be run out of town as a crook and a dodo, and yet this same dodge has worked beautifully for Republicans in Washington, who have clubbed their hapless opponents over the head with God and Old Glory and then set up shop in the Capitol and profited mightily.

It was Republicans, who oppose government intrusion, who brought forth the remarkably insane Broadcast Decency Enforcement Act that makes broadcasters liable for fines of up to $500,000 for any "obscene, indecent, or profane" material, whatever that may mean. It was brought forth in the wake of the singer Janet Jackson's nipple appearing on national television during halftime of a Super Bowl game. As interpreted by the FCC, it is okay to say *dickhead*, indecent to say *bullshit*. This is horse hockey of a high order. The word *indecent* can be interpreted so many ways that a radio station in Lexington, Kentucky, decided to cancel a radio show of mine because I used the word *breast*. Here in the land of the free, freedom won by brave men whose speech was salty and whose interest in women was keen, a man cannot say *breast* on the radio. How do these people manage to order fried chicken at a restaurant?

The Republicans deposed Mr. DeLay in time for this year's elections. When you're a Jet and the spit hits the fan, you've got brothers around, you're a family man, but if your ball-bearing eyes don't photograph well and you've raised truckloads of cash by putting the screws to the fat cats until they squeaked and you got Indian tribes to pay for you and yours to fly to Scotland and play golf—if you tend to scare the bejeebers out of people and you gerrymandered Texas to squeeze more Republicans into Congress because you are a majority leader who knows that one can never have too much majority—the moment they sensed that he was wounded, those timid Republicans who kissed his ring at prayer breakfasts and waved the flies away from his scrambled eggs and sausage, they threw him out the window. They threw their daddy out the window.

Politics can be merciless. Jimmy Carter will never live down having used the word *malaise*—it will be in his bio forever. Bill Clinton had sex with that woman and they will be linked forever. Poor Dick Cheney fired a barrel of buckshot into the face of a 78-year-old Texas lawyer and this cartoon image (BLAMMO!!!) is now a permanent part of his legacy. Poor Ronald Reagan fell asleep in staff meetings and sometimes forgot where he was and why. A genial man who did many good things but Americans will always know him as the president of dementia. Mr. Nixon was done in by his own staff who decided not to burn the tapes, and so the statesman who made the Great Turn toward China suffered the humiliation of being quoted accurately when he was talking drunken talk about Jews and liberals and the eastern establishment. LBJ was a tragic figure in the four years left to him after he left office, gulping nitro pills, haunted by the millstone of Vietnam.

And then there is Mr. Bush. One can debate whether he is the lousiest president in our history or the first or second runner-up to Warren G. Harding or James Buchanan, or only worthy of dishonorable mention. He tried to look like Harry Truman and he came out closer to Truman Capote. Petulant, vain, devious, enormously talented, and in the end, meant to be forgotten. Whoever designs his library, don't make the parking lot too big.

A good Democrat named Al Gore
Lost the battle after winning the war
When old Karl Rove
Stole the pies from the stove—
And look who walked through the door—
Mr. Bush's ne'er do well son—
He snuck through the courtroom and won,
And we liberals collapsed
And wept in our Pabst
For the dark deeds that had been done.

HOMEGROWN
DEMOCRAT

★

Chapter 1

DON'T THINK
YOU'RE SPECIAL

Here's to Vice-President Cheney
Who is neither charming nor brainy,
But he's doing his best,
He's avoided arrest,
And he's been careful with his gun, ain't he.

I AM a Democrat, which was nothing I decided for myself but simply the way I was brought up, starting with the idea of *Don't take all the cookies, even though nobody is looking. Think about the others. Do unto them as you would have them do unto you,* which is the basis of the simple social compact by which we live. And also *You are not so different from other people so don't give yourself airs—God isn't going to make an exception in your case so don't ask,* which was drummed into us children back in the old days when everyone attended public school, except Catholics, Rockefellers, or boys with behavior problems. In seventh-grade phys ed class, you faced up to that harrowing moment when you shed your skivvies and stepped bare naked into a shower room with thirty other boys, some plump ones, some thin as a rail, very few Greek gods among them, moist pink flesh stepping gingerly to a showerhead, soaping up, rinsing, getting the hell out and into your clothes. A democratic moment. There was the outhouse experience, sitting and dropping your dirt into a hole and hearing it plop on other people's. Our house had indoor plumbing, which permitted greater delicacy in these matters, but up on the farm, you sat in the old two-holer and perhaps were joined by a cousin. At first you pretended that you had only come to peruse the Sears catalog and its fine selection of sporting goods, but then gravity took its course, your bowels opened, a great stink was launched downward, and you were initiated into the great democracy of the latrine: *WE ALL DO IT.*

The democracy of public school was powerful. *Don't be conceited. Wait your turn. Keep your voice down.* The democracy of the gospel. *All have sinned and come short of the glory of God. All we like sheep have gone astray.* The democracy of work. *Do your part. Pull your weight. Don't jerk people around just because you can.* And so when I attend the big Labor Day picnic on Harriet Island in St. Paul, I am among civilized people who grew up with those rules, and when I find myself at a big corporate gala, I feel suffocated, surrounded by loud, self-absorbed, and rather brutal people. You sit in first class on an airplane and the proportion of assholes is high. Power corrupts and it also makes for bad manners. But democratic faith, plus our common tongue and a fondness for jokes and the romance of American landscape and history, binds us together. America is a mystical union of souls tied each to the other by invisible bonds, by rhythm and twang, a love of corn, a belief in equality.

This union, sacred to Lincoln, was made holy by the blood sacrifice of the heroic dead at Gettysburg, Verdun, Normandy, Anzio, Inchon, Da Nang, Kuwait, Kabul, Baghdad, not by the brilliance of generals or the honesty of the public officials who sent the heroes to war, but by the love and loyalty of the dead, and so the union endures, despite greed and corruption, despite the grandiosity of cranks on the radio and the flummery of e-z idea salesmen and the enormous cheat that the Conservative Revolution has turned out to be.

This union was not so clear to me when I was young and immortal and full of intense vapors, but now I am part of the democracy of old age, forgetful about car keys and glasses, no longer bounding up stairs—if we live long enough, humility is imposed on us, and we face up to the ultimate democracy of death, where the rich man met Lazarus at last after years of riding past him in the limo. I learned a little about humility in July 2001, when my mitral valve came unhinged and I was wheeled into a bright room at St. Mary's Hospital in Rochester, Minnesota, and slid onto a glassy platform and Dr. Orczulak, the son of a steelworker in Pittsburgh, sliced open my thorax and eight hours later I felt my little boat bump up on a foggy shore and a young woman named Erinn assured me that I would be okay and removed the hose from my throat and the next day my catheter was removed and that night a nurse in a blue uniform with a pager clipped to her lapel bent down to take my blood pressure and the weight of the pager opened the fabulous landscape of her breasts and my libido awakened and I realized that I would indeed survive.

I grew up among Bible-believing people in Minnesota, a cold-weather state when the wind blows down from Manitoba; it gets so cold your skin hurts, your innards clench up, and a man's testes shrink to the size of garden peas, but *Everyone else is just as cold as you are so don't complain about it, this is not a personal experience,* that's what we say, and you comfort yourself with fried eggs and bacon and you bulk up a little by spring, but everyone else puts on weight too, so it's not a problem unless you're obsessed with mirrors, which we aren't.

Here we have the democracy of flatness: there aren't many hills for rich people to build castles on top of. We suffer less from the self-esteem issues that drive people to purchase Hummers or have their faces surgically rearranged or own 300 pairs of shoes. We could do all that if we moved to Las Vegas or Phoenix or some place where nobody knows us, and maybe we will someday— win the lottery, buy a shiny new face with a cleft chin, drive around in a paramilitary vehicle with our Russian wolfhounds and give ourselves the nicknames Biff and

Muffy, but for now, here we are, and our friends and families keep us in line. *Don't get hoity-toity with us.* Your impact on the world is slight, so take life as a comedy and play it for laughs. You die, there is some grief, a momentary bowing of heads, and a few people really do suffer from your absence, but the impact on the greater world is negligible. You do not leave a big hole. They dig a hole and put you in it.

Minnesota was settled by no-nonsense socialists from Germany and Sweden and Norway who unpacked their trunks and planted trees and set about organizing schools, churches, libraries, lodges, societies and benevolent associations, brotherhoods and sisterhoods, and raised their children to Mind Your Manners, Be Useful, Pay Attention, Make Something of Yourself, Turn Down the Thermostat (If You're Cold, Go Put on a Sweater), Share and Share Alike, Be Satisfied with What You Have—a green Jell-O salad with mandarin oranges, miniature marshmallows, walnuts, and Miracle Whip is by God good enough for anybody. In school you brought a valentine for everybody on Valentine's Day and we all said the Pledge of Allegiance and sang about the land of the free and the home of the brave—the Baptists sat

down with Jews and Unitarians, the doctor's children
and the farmer's and the mechanic's, we danced the
schottische together, we taunted and were taunted. We
were taught to Be Happy with What You've Got and
Don't Think You're So Special Because You're Not. We
were inoculated against narcissism. *Spoiled* was a strong
pejorative and if it was applied to us, it stung. (I think of
spoiled rotten, I think of Rush Limbaugh, the Biggest
Ego in the East, whose self-absorption borders on the
fetal.) We were brought up to take pains to not be Special. If you drop the fly ball, you feel bad, even if your
team is nine runs behind. You are not nonchalant about
letting them down. If you hit a homer, you don't booga-
loo around the bases with your fists in the air and slide
into home—you trot modestly, head down, and walk to
the dugout and sit on the bench. If there is one meatball
left on the platter, you do not take it, you take half of it,
and someone else takes half of that and so it is endlessly
divided down to the last crumb. Not a state of show-
boats or hot dogs or motormouths. We tend not to yell
or honk unless necessary. We don't stare. We are not
uncomfortable about silence and can sit calmly and
quietly in the company of others and eat and not feel

compelled to launch into a monologue about My Day
and How I Triumphed over Cunning Adversaries. Silence, the purest democracy. The sweetest part of Sunday
morning: when the organ stops and nobody speaks and
we look at the light streaming in the windows.

I live in Minnesota for the plain and simple reason
that *I am not so different from these people* and I want
my daughter to feel that she is one of them too. And because the social compact is still intact here, despite Republicans trying to unscrew it and put it up for auction.

Here in St. Paul, I live a few blocks from where my
mother lived back in the Dirty Thirties when she was a
slim, shy, lovely teenager attending St. Paul Central and
hoping to become a registered nurse and earning her
keep by going door-to-door in the neighborhood selling
freshly baked peanut butter cookies in little brown paper bags. It's also the neighborhood of F. Scott Fitzgerald's boyhood, who wrote plays and got his chums to
perform them, with himself in the starring role. He re-
turned here from New York in 1919, broke, his back to
the wall, and squatted in his parents' attic and rewrote
his first novel, the one that made him famous a year

later. When it was accepted by Scribners, he dashed into the street and stopped cars and told everybody. In this way, as in others—his romantic gassiness, his big sense of Destiny, his wild behavior—he distanced himself from us. We think he would've been better off had he married a St. Paul girl, bought a house on Goodrich Avenue, and simply written the fiction and not tried to live it.

*

For all that's changed since then, a good deal has not—people still say *please* and *excuse me* and *good morning* and hold the door open for you and indulge the free spirits among us though it's irksome when their dandelions go to seed and blow onto our land. We try to shovel the sidewalks in the winter for the greater good. If you're in the mood, you can make small talk with us and we will make small talk back. The art of small talk is beautiful and intricate and hard for foreigners to learn. It does not preclude large talk. You could be waiting for the Grand Avenue bus with a man you've seen around the neighborhood over the years, at the dry cleaner's and Kowalski's and Tom the tailor's and La Cucaracha, and ask him how he's doing and he'll tell you about the death of his father in the hospital the night before and you will listen to his spontaneous monologue and ease his loneliness a little. An utterly common occurrence in a society that isn't hung up on social status—people turning to each other and dishing up a story of astonishing frankness and intimacy.

In the new privatized, low-tax, minimal-services society the Republicans are striving to lay on us, public transportation will offer no pleasure whatsoever. The bus will be for losers and dopes. The driver will sit in a bulletproof box and there will be no conversation with him. Or with the angry and sullen passengers, people who have lost hope that their kids can rise in the world and have a better life, which is the hope that makes it possible for me to turn to you and say something about the weather. Civility leads to civilities. In Republican America, you will avoid public life whenever possible. Stay in your car, keep the doors locked. The public library, that great democratic temple, will become a waiting room for desperate and broken people, the alkies, the whacked-out, the unemployables, and the public schools will become holding tanks for children whose parents were too unresourceful to find good schools for them, and politics will be so ugly and rancid that decent people will avoid expressing an opinion for fear of being screeched at and hectored and spat on. The antitax fanatics will rain their abuse on elected officials, the religious right will carry on their little wars, and gradually the bureaucrats will get tired and retreat, the handsome downtown will dwindle, the city fall into sad neglect.

That isn't the country I grew up in, dear hearts.

I grew up north of Minneapolis, along the Mississippi, and at the age of 12, rode my bike past the truck farms and cornfields of Brooklyn Park and into the bustling city, the lumberyards and salvage yards along Washington Avenue, the printing plants, binderies, machine shops, the barrel works, foundries, dairy, meatpacking houses, the factories along the Soo Line and Great Northern tracks, the tanneries and breweries and bottling plant, a world of work and me coasting by on a summer day, pedaling toward the great towers of downtown, Dayton's department store, the theaters on Hennepin Avenue, and the stone castle of a public library. I had no lock for my bike. I leaned it against a wall and walked into a Fort Knox of books and stayed for hours.

The country still remembered the Great Depression

and that memory united us. My mother recalled when hobos came to the back door for a handout and you fed them. Gypsies came around, selling brooms. You brushed elbows with bums when you sang with your church group at the Union Gospel Mission and you pressed the flesh with Cedric Adams, the voice of the *Noontime News* who sat in the WCCO booth at the State Fair and hobnobbed. You picked up hitchhikers, who might be college boys or migrant farmhands heading to Fargo for the wheat harvest. Hitchhiking was a civil tradition of the Thirties that lingered on into the Sixties, now utterly vanished. We do not trust each other today. We used to and we don't anymore. The urban legend about razor blades in apples given to trick-or-treaters at Halloween was pure fiction but it closed the door on the idea of offering children any home-baked goods or fruit on this sweet occasion. One episode of product poisoning led to a frenzy of safety seals. We live in a country of distrust. I miss the old one.

*

There were certain points back then where all roads led and everybody came together, nabob and yahoo, poet and redneck, Baptist and Catholic, and the public school was one of those places. In Anoka, Minnesota, some children wound up at Dartmouth and Stanford and Carleton and Princeton but they spent their formative years in the public school system with the children of farmers and carpenters and cops and firemen. They all rode together on the big yellow school bus and cheered for the Tornadoes and ate macaroni and cheese in the lunchroom. This experience is valuable. It gives you a tribal feeling. Everybody else knows the same songs you do, including *Nobody likes me, everybody hates me, guess I'll go eat worms* and *Did you ever think as the hearse rolls by that you may be the next to die?* And the one about the doctor and the nurse and the lady with the alligator purse. And *Minnesota, hats off to thee, to your colors true we shall ever be* and maybe *All glory, laud, and honor to Thee O Savior King, to Whom the lips of children made sweet hosannas ring*—or maybe not, there's room for diversity here—but we all grew up on the same playground and skipped rope to *Mable, Mable, set the table, she put on the red hot pepper* and played Rover, Red Rover and Prisoner's Base and Run Sheep Run and Fox and Geese and we all knew what liverwurst was and Cheez Whiz and Spam and we all knew the story of Daniel in the lion's den and Noah's Ark and the Prodigal Son and a couple of hundred other basic tales. I'd hate to think that little Hmong and Mexican children might go through the St. Paul public schools and not learn *O say can you see any bedbugs on me* and *On top of Old Smokey all covered with sand, I shot my poor teacher with a big rubber band* and *Mine eyes have seen the glory of the burning of the school.* And of course *Step on a crack and break your mother's back.* Thanks to this wise saying, millions of youngsters have learned something about mercy and also avoided tripping on cracks and skinning their knees.

My wife and I lived in New York City for a while, a gorgeous place if you like people, but then we begat a little girl, and we brought her home to Minnesota so she could have aunts and uncles and grow up among soft-spoken people. My people. I attended the University of Minnesota and remember the marching band blazing down University Avenue, flags snapping in the wind, the *shap-shap-shap* of their shoes, drums pounding out the cadence, and wheeling into Memorial Stadium packed with 61,000 people and when we stood and sang *firm and strong, united are we,* you could feel that union in your shoes as thousands of gold balloons rose in the October air and you felt blessed to be one of this hardy northern tribe, honest and true, camped along the Mississippi River and the world's largest freshwater lake, the state that produced the Mayo Clinic, Sinclair Lewis, Hubert Humphrey, Arvonne Fraser, Gene McCarthy, Robert Bly, Herb Brooks, Charles Schulz, Bill Holm, and Jessica Lange. I want my daughter to be from here too. As the song says, *Like the stream that bends to sea, like the pine that seeks the blue, Minnesota still for thee, thy sons and daughters true.* When I stand at a urinal, it's the thought of Minnehaha Falls that loosens the sphincter, and when I need to sleep at night, it's the 87 counties of Minnesota that I slowly recite and I drop off around Pennington, Pipestone, Polk, Pope, Ramsey. Which is where St. Paul is, a Democratic stronghold— so there is a high value placed on public services. If you call 911 in St. Paul, the cops or the EMTs will arrive within four minutes. In the Republican suburbs, where No New Taxes is the beginning and end of politics, the response time can be anywhere between ten or fifteen and thirty minutes, and if the elephant steps on your chest, good luck, pal.

This is the difference between Democrats and Republicans these days, when it comes right down to it. Republicans wrap themselves in Old Glory and talk about school prayer and the sanctity of marriage but when it comes to providing services, you shouldn't get your hopes up. They might send an ambulance or they might just send a get-well card. In yellow-dog St. Paul, you will be rescued by the St. Paul fire department and there is no better emergency service anywhere in the civilized world. You may be flat on the floor feeling as if an elephant stepped on your chest, or your child may have swallowed a fistful of God knows what medication, or your grandma may have slipped on the ice and banged her noggin and she insists she's okay but in Swedish— whatever your dilemma, the St. Paul rescue squad will deal with it in swift and professional fashion. Because we Democrats feel that the people of St. Paul are entitled to the best when it comes to what's crucial. You can be a Christian, atheist, Buddhist, nudist, and the rescue squad will be there for you within four minutes.

Republicans have become the antigovernment party. Government is the problem, not the solution. They forget that most people who enter public service are propelled by a desire to do good. This altruism is especially powerful among the uniformed services, cops, firemen, EMTs—read *102 Minutes* (Jim Dwyer and Kevin Flynn) about the cops and firemen who raced to the Twin Towers when the planes hit—they raced in from Brooklyn and Queens, guys who were off duty suddenly came on duty, all over the Northeast men reached for the car keys—but Republicans don't go for do-gooders and would be content to disband the police and outsource the work. If they could save a nickel, they'd have you calling a 911 operator in Bangalore.

*

Republicans have perfectly nice manners, normal hair, pleasant smiles, good deodorants, but when it comes right down to it, you don't want them monitoring your oxygen flow: they will set it to the minimum required to sustain basic brain function, and then hand you a prayer card. There are reality-based Republicans whom I would trust completely, but those aren't the ones riding high in Washington. They are a party that is all about perception, the Christian party that conceals enormous malice, led by brilliant bandits who are dividing and conquering. They rushed a law through Congress to keep a brain-dead woman alive in Florida and created a circus around her comatose body and then, when polls showed the winds against them, quietly folded their tents and crept away. Remarkable. We Democrats may fade, lose heart, languish, but we don't abandon the fort.

Chapter 2

WE HAVE BECOME THE
TEDIOUS CONSERVATIVES

There once was a good Democrat
Who was able to talk through his hat.
Such smart things he said
Off the top of his head
Or else out the place where he sat.

SOMETHING has gone seriously haywire with the Republican Party. Once, it was the party of pragmatic Main Street businessmen in steel-rimmed spectacles who decried profligacy and waste, were devoted to sensible long-term thinking and the good of their communities, and supported the sort of prosperity that raises all ships. They were no-nonsense fellows who prided themselves on their Spartan discipline. They were savers, investors, planners, not big spenders and stuffed shirts. They preferred a gray metal desk in a plain office with a linoleum floor to the farcical grandeur of the CEO suite and they didn't gouge out windfall profits for themselves by plunging the company into a junkyard of debt. They were honorable, good-hearted men, as different from Dick Cheney as Beethoven is from Norman Bates. They had vanquished the gnarlier elements of their party, the Roosevelt-haters, the flat-earth folks and Prohibitionists, the Know-Nothings, the McCarthyites. The genial Eisenhower was their man, a genuine American hero of D-Day, who made it okay for reasonable people to vote Republican (even in the South), and he brought the Korean War to a stalemate, produced the Interstate Highway System, declined to rescue the French colonial army in Vietnam, and gave us a period of peace and prosperity, in which (oddly) American arts and letters flourished mightily and higher education burgeoned and there was a degree of plain decency in the country. Fifties Republicans were giants compared to today's. Richard Nixon was the last Republican leader to feel a Christian obligation toward the poor. He was the patron of the National Endowment for the Arts and the Environmental Protection Agency, the man who opened the door to China.

In the years between Nixon and the Chief Occupant of today, the party migrated southward down the Twisting Trail of Gas-Powered Rhetoric and sneered at the idea of public service and became the Scourge of Liberalism, the Great Crusade against the Sixties, the Death Star of Government, while carrying on bold symbolic forays that stunned and fascinated the media by their sheer chutzpah, such as the misty-eyed patriotism of Ronald Reagan who, while George McGovern flew bombers in World War II, took a pass and made training films in Long Beach. The Willie Horton ads of 1988. The flogging of the undeserving poor, the carefully coded racism, the drumbeat of diatribes against the Gummint. The Nixon moderate vanished like the passenger pigeon, purged by a legion of angry white men who had risen to power on pure punk politics, nasty, violent, borderline sociopath. "*Bipartisanship* is another term for date rape," says Grover Norquist, the Sid Vicious of the GOP. "I don't want to abolish government. I simply want to reduce it to the size where I can drag it into the bathroom and drown it in the bathtub." The boy has Oedipal problems and government is his daddy.

The party of Lincoln and Liberty was transmogrified

into the party of hairy-backed swamp developers and corporate shills, fundamentalist bullies, Christians of convenience, hobby cops, misanthropic frat boys, cigar monkeys, ninja dittoheads, shrieking midgets, tax cheats, cheese merchants, cat stranglers, goldbrickers, gun fetishists, pill pushers, chronic nappers, nihilists in golf pants, backed-up Baptists, bozos on horseback, panjandrums of Ponzi marketing and the grand pooh-bahs of Percodan, mouth breathers and tongue thrusters, testosterone junkies, oversexed hedgehogs, brownshirts in pinstripes, sweatshop tycoons, line jumpers, randy preachers, marsupial moms and chirpy news anchors, UFO scholars, shroomheads, hacks, fakirs, aggressive dorks, wizened aliens, aluminum siding salesmen, little honkers out to diminish the rest of us, braying, smirking, scratching on the national blackboard, Newt's evil spawn, disciples of their Etch A Sketch president with a voice like a dial tone, a rigid, incurious, isolated man, not much introspection going on here, no inquiring minds eager to learn about the world, not much chance of anyone picking up a book not on the official reading list and hearing a still small voice, a dull and rigid man suspicious of the free flow of information and of secular institutions in general, whose philosophy is a jumble of badly sutured slogans trying to walk, whose millions of supporters are awakening to the damage this man has done to our country. George Bush: the No. 1 reason why the rest of the world thinks we're deaf, dumb, and dangerous.

What gorgeous characters they have given us, a cast worthy of Dickens—the oily and toxic DeLay, the lubricious Lott, the bland and arrogant Dr. Frist, the shabby and devious Rove, the prim and chill Miz Rice, the meathead Hastert, the hapless Miers, the squinty Rumsfeld, the Obersturmbannführer Cheney, and the tragic Powell, the Company Man who could have been great but deferred to the Boss's Callow Son, the Young Pretender. Rich ironies abound! Lies pop up like toadstools in the forest! Wild swine crowd round the public trough! Outrageous gerrymandering! Districts shaped like orthopedic devices! Pocket lining on a massive scale! Extortion, bribery, lavish gifts, the Choctaw Indians of Mississippi and the Coushattas of Louisiana reamed for all they are worth! Cash payments to maintain the sweatshops of the Marianas! K Street lobbyists sit in the committee rooms and write legislation to alleviate the suffering of billionaires! Regulatory agencies are handed over to the paid minions of the industries regulated! Let the mine owners run the safety board and hire the inspectors! Turn the forests over to the logging companies! Give the public airwaves to the conglomerates! Give the emergency management agency to Joe's friend from the Arabian Horse Federation! Young Republicans riding the government gravy train! The train is full! More cars are added! Hypocrisies shine like cat turds in the moonlight! O Mark Twain, where art thou at this hour? Arise, and behold the Gilded Age reincarnated gaudier than ever, upholding great wealth as the sure sign of divine grace, railing against the expense of public schools and calling for more prisons. Henry Mencken, you poisoned these boobs and they've come back hardier than ever. A whole new strain, more virulent than any previous.

Every satirist who drew breath has flung pots of ink at this parade of tooting lummoxes and here it is come round again, marching down Main Street, fat, red-faced, sporting plumes and sashes, their chests glittering with self-awarded medals, waving Old Glory as if they owned it, hail, hail, the gang's all here, ta-ra-ra-BOOM-de-ay.

*

Somehow it happened. The old GOP was shouldered aside. Nixon was shamed and renters took over his party and trashed it. Anarchists called themselves conservatives. So we liberals must take over the job. Once we were young and rebellious and lobbed eggs at the bewigged and berobed Establishment and now we're the parents with the thankless job of home maintenance, defending principles that go back to the founding of the republic, namely, the notion of the common good, the principle of equality, the very idea of representative government. We've become the tiresome, repetitive old dad who tells his boys that Progress Depends on Teamwork and All of Us Learning to Pull Together, while the Republicans have turned into the Screw-You Party. They tore into the progressive income tax, raked the IRS over the coals for chasing down deadbeats, and succeeded in convincing the American people that they are overtaxed, so that 17% of Americans now believe it is justifiable to cheat on your income tax. This is a big change in ethics.

George W. Bush, elected to office by the late Justice Rehnquist, led America into the single greatest failure of national defense in our history, the attacks of

September 11, 2001, in which nineteen men with box cutters brought us into national shock, a monumental failure the details of which the White House fought to keep secret, even as it ran the country into debt up to the hubcaps, thanks to generous tax cuts for the well-fixed, even as it engaged in a preemptive war against a small country that did not seek war with us, which was sold to the American public on the basis of brazen lies, a war that was horribly mismanaged, plunging the Iraqi people into year after year of near anarchy, exposing American troops to relentless guerrilla opposition, expendable American kids from poor rural families. And then there is the matter of war crimes.

Abu Ghraib. Guantánamo. Secret prisons in the Middle East that our torture victims were outsourced to. One prisoner, Mohammed al-Qahtani, held naked in isolation under bright lights for months, threatened by dogs, subjected to unbearable noise, held underwater, and otherwise abused, so that he begged to be allowed to kill himself. When the Senate approved the Torture Convention in 1994, it defined torture as an act "specifically intended to inflict severe physical or mental pain or suffering." The administration defied Congress to enforce the law and Congress harrumphed and turned away. And so young American men and women, under pain of court-martial, are ordered to do disgusting things to helpless prisoners that might, should circumstances change in a few years, get them hauled up for war crimes, and if they are, they will not be joined in the dock by Secretary Rumsfeld or President Bush.

The only word that describes this is *evil*.

A career based on creating low expectations keeps sinking lower and lower. The national disgrace that was Katrina. The famous headline that said, BUSH: ONE OF THE WORST DISASTERS TO HIT THE U.S. Hungry black people huddled together in the Superdome, stretched out asleep between the goal lines, and a 911 operator broke into sobs telling what it was like to talk to little kids in flooded houses and tell them help was on the way when she knew very well that it wasn't—that *until they realized it would be shown on national television, the administration didn't give a rip what happened to New Orleans.*

Meanwhile, an enormous transfer of wealth is taking place in this country, money siphoning out of the commonwealth and flowing upward into the bank accounts of the fortunate and well-situated. The top 1% holds nearly half the financial wealth, the greatest concentration of wealth of any industrialized nation, more concentrated than at any time since the Depression. In 1980, on average, CEOs earned 42 times the salary of the average worker, and these days they earn about 476 times that salary. Since 1980, the rich have been getting richer fast and furiously and hardworking people in the middle are sliding down the greasy slope who never imagined this could happen to them. The concentration of wealth and power in the hands of a few is the death knell of democracy. No republic in the history of humankind has survived this. We will decide what happens to ours. The omens are not good. So far we care more about amusement than about the future. We would trade our children for a bigger car and our grandchildren for a Florida condo.

*

I am a liberal and liberalism is the politics of kindness. Liberals stand for tolerance, magnanimity, community spirit, the defense of the weak against the powerful, love of learning, freedom of belief, art and poetry, city life, the very things that make America worth dying for. Republicans stand for tax cuts, deregulation, and providing good service to their clients. Their symbol is the $223 million bridge almost as long as the Golden Gate that will link the town of Ketchikan, Alaska (population 8,000)—a town that exists to sell T-shirts and postcards to cruise passengers for three months a year—to the city airport on Gravina Island, replacing a seven-minute ferry ride. And the billion-dollar two-mile-long bridge to connect Anchorage to hundreds of square miles of undeveloped wetlands. Banditry, in other words.

Meanwhile, squeeze the poor as hard as possible. Dump their problems onto the states. Cut taxes. Use the refund to buy a gun and an attack dog to take with you when you drive your all-terrain vehicle through the barricades of Republicanville to make a foray into enemy territory to purchase supplies. They are leading this great land toward a loose confederation of tribes where Social Security and Medicare will be dim memories—where Baptists will take care of their own and Unitarians will retreat to Vermont. There will be red and blue occupation zones, and America will become a series of malls connected by interstates, and people will live in walled compounds with moats, like in the Middle Ages.

Other liberals, bless their bleeding hearts, are deeply

into diversity and multiculturalism—today is Hmong Day and tomorrow we'll make a teepee and next week we'll learn to tango—and so the public school doesn't use the word *Christmas* without mentioning Kwanzaa, Hanukkah, and Ramadan in the same sentence. But I am more interested in middleness and centrality and ordinariness and the sense of *America* that we are losing in the Bush regime. He is leading us down the old plank road toward Plantation Days in Dixie, where you are either landed aristocracy or a supervisor or a barefoot field hand in overalls. This is not the America I grew up in.

What we must conserve is the middle class: the stable family that can afford to enjoy music and theater and take the kids to Europe someday and put money in the collection plate and save for college and keep up the home and be secure against catastrophe. This family has taken big hits in payroll taxes and loss of buying power and a certain suppressed panic about job security. Their children have lost hope of achieving the good life their parents and grandparents have; they expect to slide into debt to pay for a mediocre education, get a minimum-wage job, live in Mom's basement, and slide into their thirties. No wonder they're depressed and resort to alcohol and devastating drugs. "You going to party?" they say, and for them *party* means "drink until unconscious." When I walk past college bars at night and see beautiful young women vomiting between parked cars, I wish Mr. Bush were there to hold their heads.

The middle class is losing its optimism and good humor and if Democrats don't defend it, it could be washed away along with the old-fashioned notion of the common good that was strong back in my youth in the Fifties when we thought of this as one nation. We learned it in public school from the Declaration of Independence and the Gettysburg Address. America is predicated on an idea, which is equality, and the equal right to life, liberty, and the pursuit of happiness. We are not a herd of woolly mammoths united only for self-preservation, nor a gang of mercenaries, nor the United Federation of Caucasians or the Church of the Sacred Banner, we are a noble political experiment and when Lincoln rose on that November afternoon in 1863, after a man with three names had blown hard for two hours, he summed up in two minutes the great cause: what could be the Lord's purpose in allowing the green fields of Pennsylvania to be soaked with blood and gore if not to consecrate these United States to the ideal of government of and by and for the people?

Nothing in literature moved me in my youth so much as the Civil War, the Bruce Catton histories, the letters of soldiers, the Brady photographs, Whitman's *Specimen Days*, the grace and gravity of Mr. Lincoln, the story of the First Minnesota that charged forward to plug a hole at Gettysburg and save the Union line from folding—the whole epic sweep of the war and the cavalier arrogance of the South that pushed the nation to conflict and that almost put to rout the muddling patriots of the North, the stubbornness of Grant, the cult worship of Lee, the woozy romantic twaddle of the Lost Cause, and the mystical sense of *Union* that rose from the slaughter. A house divided cannot stand. Slavery was a gross insult to the national ideal; we could not tolerate it and still be the United States.

If the powerful have free rein to stomp on the weak, then the Union itself is weakened: to tolerate injustice will corrupt politics and leach away public happiness and darken the arena. Walking the mean streets we will regard each other with blank suspicion. We will keep the gates locked, install new gates, hire private security guards, give free rein to paranoia, and thereby make of each American home a little prison in which our children feed on video stimuli and are denied actual experience in the world.

The Union does not rest on strength of arms or financial wealth but on the common faith of American people that their children have a fair chance to thrive, that the iron gates have not slammed shut on them, that there is justice, that the Bill of Rights has not been privatized. This is the bottom line in America: we have to feel that our kids stand a chance—otherwise, there's a civil war brewing.

We are one country, and I remain a proud Unionist, happy to sing "The Star-Spangled Banner" and pledge allegiance, sing about the amber waves of grain, wish I was in the land of cotton, pick my teeth with a carpet tack, be in the kitchen with Dinah, hate to see the evening sun go down, take myself out to the ball game, walk that lonesome valley, and lean on the everlasting arms. I love this country. All it needs is some true loyalty, the kind that doesn't accept bullies. Look at how the national anthem has been abused over the years by little pop tarts and divas wailing on it at ball games until people come to assume it's an unsingable soprano showpiece, but when you put "The

Star-Spangled Banner" into the key of G, the people's key, the crowd throws back their heads and sings with all their hearts. They love this country. This is one of those simple dumb discoveries a man makes, like the December night I came out of the New York hospital where I, a bystander at my wife's travail, had held my naked newborn six-pound shining-eyed daughter in my hands. In a daze, a father again at 55, I walked around midtown Manhattan at midnight stunned by the utter ordinariness, *everybody comes into the world pretty much like that.* In the same spirit, late at night, after the climb to the hill of sexual delight and the quiet clamor of joy, you lie and think, *It's like this for all of the others too. Up in Frogtown and down on the West Side, and in Minneapolis, men and women are dancing in the dark just like this.* In the same spirit, I walk around St. Paul and think, *This is a great country and it wasn't made so by angry right-wingers.* You can sit beside the Mississippi and look up at Masqueray's cathedral and enjoy the same sunshine as everyone else and invite your grand ambition and feel that by the grace of God your chances are acceptably good.

We have a sacred duty to bequeath this country to our grandchildren in better shape than however we found it. We have a long way to go and we're not getting any younger.

The Union is what needs defending against this confederacy of Republicans who have humbugged us to death on terrorism and tax cuts for the rich and school prayer and flag burning and claimed the right to dump their sewage upstream from town and clear-cut the forest and gut the IRS and take over the public airwaves and to know what books we read and to hell with anybody who opposes them. And their victory has been accompanied by such hubris as would choke a goat. One Republican columnist wrote that Democrats should give up opposing tax breaks for the rich because working people don't vote their self-interest, they vote their aspirations and are happy to give big gifts to rich people because they hope to become rich too. A small-bore TV Republican named Tucker Carlson wrote a column saying that if Democrats want to win, they need to (1) talk tough, (2) start their own think tanks, and (3) get a sense of humor—(3) got one, Tucker, (2) got plenty of think tanks, except we call them colleges, and (1) shut your piehole, pea brain, or I'll light your loafers.

Democrats have changed America in basic ways in

the past fifty years that have benefited everyone. Race has become less and less an issue in people's lives and racism has ceased to be socially acceptable anywhere. Women have moved into every realm of government, business, and organizational life and this is generally accepted without comment. If you can't be comfortable around people unlike you, you're considered odd. If you pay blind allegiance to power, you're considered a dullard. We agree that children should enjoy as nearly equal opportunity in school as possible, including children with disabilities. There is general agreement on the right to a dignified old age. Democrats led the way in bringing these things about. It's one thing to get into power and do favors for your friends; it's quite another to touch the conscience of a nation.

Democrats are accused of having no new ideas but when you look at Republican ideology, which is the guarantee of the right to be a jerk, then the old American idea of a decent democratic society starts to look better and better.

Chapter 3

WHERE I'M COMING FROM

Here is to Barack Obama
Who has a black dad and white mama.
He can rock, he can bop,
And yet he will stop
To participate in Bowlerama.

I WAS BORN in 1942, in time to catch glimpses of fugi-
tive scenes from the 19th century and get coal smoke
in my nostrils and hear the *oomph* of steam engines in
the night and the scream of their whistles. Somber
women in plain print dresses walked through my childhood quoting proverbs (*haste makes waste; if wishes
were horses, then beggars would ride and the world be
drowned in a sea of pride*) and wooden-faced men who
kept a heavy-lidded watch on things. I rode the hayrack

37

drawn by Belgian horses, harness jingling, tossing their heads, and once I rode one bareback, clinging to his mane, pure glory at the age of four. I stood next to Uncle Jim, his forehead against the flank of a cow, and smelled the warm milk squirting into the steel bucket and poured it into a milk can to be lowered into a cold cistern in the milk house. I chased chickens through the lilac bushes and grabbed their ankles with a coat hanger and brought them to the chopping block to be dispatched with an ax. On Sunday mornings, I sat on hard wooden chairs next to stern old white-bearded Plymouth Brethren in black gabardine suits and white starched shirts buttoned to the top, no ties, no vain adornments, who walked the narrow path of truth and righteousness, intent on finding the Lord's Will for their lives; they put Him first and material things second, as a result of which they lived on the fringes of society, which was more or less what Jesus had promised His followers, so they were not disappointed. They were not much for small talk and they didn't trust strangers or confide in them. On their best days, they were funny and generous and joyful, and on their worst days, they could be cold and spiteful. They were stubborn stoics who got up at dawn and washed their faces in cold water from steel basins and read a chapter of Scripture and prayed at length and then worked until dusk and had supper and toddled off to bed early. They bought no insurance and had no faith in doctors. They accepted disease as their lot in life and pain to be cheerfully endured and they walked down the narrow road that life assigned them, walked to the end knowing it was not the end but only a corner around which Christ awaited them in shining glory, His loving arms open to receive them. They were people of profound kindness. God had instructed them to be such, and so they were.

I am descended from an act of kindness. My grandfather James Keillor journeyed from New Brunswick to Minnesota in 1880 to help out his brother-in-law who had homesteaded north of Anoka and was dying of tuberculosis. (James's grandfather Thomas Keillor came over to Canada from Yorkshire in 1773 and tried to make a living harvesting hay in the saltwater meadows that French settlers had been driven from, and here the Keillors met up with the Crandalls, who had fled north from the Connecticut colonies in 1778, having taken a stand for law and order at the wrong moment in history and lost their homes, everything they couldn't haul away in a wagon.) James was 20, a strapping young shipwright with a square jaw and handsome mustache, and he arrived in Anoka to find the brother-in-law on his deathbed, the sister with three small children and a modest farm on a sandy hill along Trott Brook in Ramsey Township. James stayed to raise those children, and then, at the age of 46, fell in love with a 20-year-old teacher, Dora Powell, whose schoolhouse was across the road from the farm. One day, he crossed the road and told her he wanted to kiss her, and he did, or she did, or something happened between them, and they were married by a justice, and he brought her home. In his hurry to get upstairs he forgot his team of horses, and they stood there all night in harness. From this passionate union sprang a whole crowd of Keillors including me.

I was born in Anoka in 1942, early enough to see horse-drawn plowing and experience the darkness of a nonelectrified farm and late enough to be only 13 when Elvis blew into town, condemned by ministers and politicians and all serious right-thinking people—as was Jerry Lee Lewis who shook our nerves and rattled our brains. I got to hear the Brethren singing a cappella the mournful old hymns (*When I survey the wondrous cross on which the Lord of glory died*) and baptize young people in Trott Brook and I saw the last living veteran of the Union army, Albert Woolson, ride in the Anoka Halloween parade, an ancient cadaverous man sunk deep in the backseat of a convertible and waving a flag in his tiny translucent hand, and I got to hear Jack Benny on the radio, but I was still young enough when John F. Kennedy ran for president to be bowled over by him.

Grandma lived on the family farm with Uncle Jim and they didn't read the paper or listen to the radio much. They had chores to do and when they'd done all they could do, they sat and visited with relatives and that was their rest. Uncle Jim had a crystal radio receiver in his room but I don't recall them ever discussing politics. Presidents came and went, and the great and famous, on a stage very far away from their thoughts. (In 1961, the year before Grandma died, I made her sit down and watch John Glenn's rocket blast into orbit, but nothing could make her believe it was true. Pictures held no truth for her, and Walter Cronkite was nobody she believed whatsoever; after all, she'd never met him.)

My dad had left the farm when he was 23 and eloped with my mother and went to work at Uncle Lew's Pure Oil station and then in the post office. In 1943 the Army took him and he fought the war in New York City, billeted in a hotel on lower Broadway, marching uptown every morning to the Army Post Office. After the war, he bought an acre of cornfield five miles north of Minneapolis and started building us a house with money borrowed under the GI Bill of Rights. We were living in south Minneapolis. Big yellow streetcars with cane seats rumbled down Bloomington Avenue past our house and we rode the trolley to Como Zoo and the great glass-domed Conservatory and the old green wooden ballpark to see the Millers and to Grandpa Denham's little stucco bungalow on Oakland Avenue under the elms overarching the green yards, the peonies and marigolds, the cast-iron lawn chairs, the birdbath, the gazing globe, the trim grass—a world of perfect order, the streets numbered and the avenues alphabetical from Aldrich, Bryant, Colfax, Dupont through Washburn, Xerxes, York, and Zenith. In my memory, my movie-star-handsome dad stands in his wool overcoat, a gray fedora on his head, smiling at the Revere movie camera in Mother's hand as a streetcar passes in the summer of 1947. He smiles, like Gary Cooper. We children stand perfectly still in Grandpa's yard and then we perk up and smile—someone off-camera has told us to—and like good children we do and my sister waves.

Dad dug the basement for the new house out of clay and loam, poured concrete, lay concrete block walls, put a roof over it, and we left Minneapolis and lived in the basement for five years while he framed up the house and finished it, a three-bedroom Cape Cod, white, blue shutters, from a blueprint he'd seen in *Popular Home*. The whine of the power saw, the smell of sawdust, the rhythm of the hammer. He worked for the Railway Mail Service, sorting mail in the mail car between St. Paul and Jamestown, North Dakota, going off to work in the afternoon, in overalls, with a government-issue .38 revolver in a holster, and put in a 12-hour shift, slept at the Cran Hotel in Jamestown, then boarded the east-bound for another shift.

To our Keillor cousins, we were city people and looked upon with some suspicion, so we tried to win their approval and pitch in with chores, shovel cow manure, do our part, not flinch. My mother, a city girl, learned to dip a dead chicken in boiling water, rip off its feathers, take a butcher knife and gut it, without comment. Though we lived in a suburb, with houses nearby, Dad once bought several crates of Leghorn chickens, brought them home, kept them overnight in the garage, and slaughtered them in the backyard in the morning. Small children came from all around to watch this. (Nobody in the Keillor family slaughters chickens anymore. A tradition has disappeared in one generation.)

*

Living in the basement, climbing the stairs to the muddy cornfield, I got my first inkling that we might be poor. Startling to a boy of six. Other people live in houses with carpets and antimacassars and dresser scarves and figurines, and we live in a bunker in the ground. *Bunker, bunk bed.* How poor are we? *I don't know.* We had a half-acre vegetable garden, corn in back, tomatoes and pole beans up front, cucumbers and squash to one side, potatoes and strawberries to the other, and in late summer Mother canned. In the laundry room stood a wall of shelves with rows of Ball fruit jars, filled with corn, beans, and stewed tomatoes. In early spring, Dad and I drove north to Lake Superior for smelting late at night: a bonfire on the shore near the mouth of the Lester River, a crowd of men in hip waders, and at reports of a run of smelt rushing for the river to spawn, the crowd waded in with landing nets and hauled up pound after pound of the little fish and we took ours home in big milk cans and filleted and froze them, to be eaten over the summer, breaded and fried. This seemed to me to be poor people food because it was free. Low-status. To Dad, of course, it was manna.

One day, helping Dad bring groceries into the basement from the car, I carried two big three-gallon glass jugs of milk, one in each hand, as I'd seen Uncle Jim carry milk cans from the barn. Toted them down the back stairs and then lost my balance, pitched forward, dropped the jugs, which broke. Six gallons of milk sploshed on the concrete floor. I picked up the shards of glass, deeply ashamed, and slunk into the room I shared with my brother and lay on my bunk and sobbed into the pillow. I had wasted food. We were poor. What would happen to us now? The pillowcase was wet with my tears. Our old black cocker spaniel, Cappadocia, lay at my feet. We were poor. On the other hand, I had books, a tablet and pencils, a radio, a pair of binoculars. Clean clothes.

When the garage got built, I liked to put a little piece of plywood on the floor and stand, bat in hand, and wait on the 3-and-2 pitch and swing, driving Whitey Ford's fastball over the centerfield fence in Yankee Stadium to win the seventh game of the World Series for the New York Giants. I earned $100,000 a year and had bought a fine home for my family, a real showplace with chandeliers, and all my aunts and uncles were proud as punch, and I had a wife, a beautiful one but vague, faraway in the stands, cheering, waving a hanky.

I sometimes tried to help Dad with building the house, but he wasn't a great teacher. He got disgusted if you made the same mistake twice. And his disgust was painful to absorb. (Those to whom ill is done do ill to others. Dad was picked on mercilessly by an older brother and he could be cruelly dismissive of his sons, and I in turn failed my own son at many turns and now I watch him with his little boys and hope the chain has run out.) On the other hand, fear of my father moved me to hole up in my room and read books, Richard Halliburton's sailing expeditions to the Far East, *Five Little Peppers and How They Grew, Black Beauty, Heidi.* And then jumped to *Main Street* and *Babbitt* and Fitzgerald and Studs Lonigan. Trying to escape my father, I escaped a career in the post office and set my sights on writing fiction. Writing was respected in our family. Not fiction necessarily, but literary endeavor was honored by my mother and father, who revered the King James Bible of course and enjoyed a clever turn of phrase in the newspaper. Mother followed Cedric Adams's tales of his boyhood in Madelia in the *Star.* Grandma had been a schoolteacher and so Keillor children were expected to succeed in school. My aunts, high school graduates all, possessed literary style, especially Aunt Eleanor, an elegant letter-writer, concise, sweet and acerbic by turns, startlingly honest at times, painstaking with descriptive detail. Writing was something of a black art, and there were bad characters in that line of work—drunkards, infidels, adulterers—but the power of language was respected. I was honored when my father asked me at age 19 to write a letter for him, setting out his qualifications to be a rural mail carrier, and I did a good workmanlike job on it, though he didn't get the position. Qualifi-cations didn't matter so much; it was political patron-age, and Dad wasn't good at that. He sent a check for $10 to Senator Ed Thye, but surely was outbid by some-one else.

My father sat at one end of the table, my mother at the other, with six children, three on a side, and we passed the stewed tomatoes, the green beans, the liver and onions, and I kept wondering, *Are we poor?* Slaugh-tering chickens seemed like a poor-person thing to do. The chickens ran like halfbacks through the lilac bushes at Grandma's farm and into the cornfield, but I ran most of them down and hooked them by the ankles with a wire hanger and brought them flapping and croaking back to Dad, who whacked them with the ax on a bloody stump. I held the carcass until it stopped dripping and gave it to Mother for defeathering and evisceration. Dad said that store-bought chicken didn't taste as good to him and Grandma said you could never be sure whether store-bought meat was properly handled. *No, it's be-cause we're poor.* On long car trips, my mother made sandwiches on a cutting board across her lap sitting in the front seat, cheese and baloney or peanut butter and jelly. She said the prices you pay for food in restaurants are outlandish. *Poor people.* Up on the farm, I washed my face with Lava soap in cold water in the morning and wiped it on a towel on a roller. I collected eggs and brought them in for breakfast, fried in a black crusted skillet on a woodstove, with a thick slice of Grandma's bread. Once I swung on a rope through the dusty air of the haymow and leaped onto a stack of bales and skidded down the side of them through the open hatch and into the bull's pen and cracked my head on his feed trough and was carried into the house and laid on the couch and Grandma put moist brown paper on the contusions and said it'd make me feel better. *We are poor people,* I thought. *We cannot afford to go to a doctor. Other people would take their children to be x-rayed after a bump on the head but in our family we put paper on them and say a prayer.*

I think of my mother at the sink peeling potatoes and looking out at the snowy garden and the wash frozen stiff on the clotheslines, and she is angry at my dad who has criticized what she spent for Christmas presents. She loves Christmas and he does not. He takes the Brethren view, that we celebrate Christ's death, not his birth, and we do so every day, and Christmas is a human institution, not of the Lord. My mother bows to puritan reasoning in principle, but she goes ahead and makes Christmas, and he accepts it, though he snipes at her for it and rolls his eyes a good deal. She defers to him, though she works as hard as he, maybe harder. She does the laundry in a washing machine with a wringer and hangs it on the line and scrubs the floors and cooks and vacuums and in late summer she takes all the bounty of the garden and cooks it in a pressure cooker to be canned in jars. You make a mistake in the canning process and you run the risk of *Clostridium botulinum*, which is so deadly that an ounce could kill 100 million people. One jar of asparagus, the equivalent of a medium-range nuclear warhead. (You tap the lid with a knife and if it rings, then the seal is good and the angel of death will pass over, and if it thuds, you throw that jar away.) She puts up a hundred jars of tomatoes and a hundred quarts of corn and makes pickles and jam, all for frugality's sake, and she doesn't remind him of the money he spends to buy a new car every few years. She can't mention this for fear he will turn silent, which is his weapon. Hers is weeping and lamentation; his is walking away and getting busy with something. She was one of those women who never read fashion magazines, never updated their look, never used hairspray, just put on a scarf. One of those women who got up every morning and got the kids off to school and did the wash and every spring went at the house in a fury of soap and Lysol and scrubbed and scraped and rendered everything shining and new and yet had not much say in things in general, having been brought up to be of service and accept a rough road without complaining, women of great kindness, creators of feasts, encouragers of children, celebrants of birthdays, confidantes. They were oppressed in the sense that many avenues were closed to them, and yet, looking back, I pity the men. We children were closer to our aunts than to our uncles, and the lives of women seemed richer to me. They were the soul of the family.

My grandma had no luxuries and no expectation of any, but her children felt the gravitational pull of prosperity. They escaped the farm and got jobs in town and bought town clothes and street shoes and didn't necessarily read Scripture after breakfast or kneel and pray, just a quick rote prayer over the food, because they had to be to work on time. They lived cheek by jowl with strangers and learned to converse with unbelievers and not bother to witness to them about the risen Christ. They bought chicken at SuperValu and got a TV set and started believing Walter Cronkite. But still they thought about God all the time. A plaque hung on our dining room wall (CHRIST THE UNSEEN GUEST AT EVERY MEAL, THE SILENT LISTENER TO EVERY CONVERSATION) to remind us that we were on His mind and after dinner we circulated the little plastic bread loaf with the Scripture verse cards and each person at the table drew a card and read a verse. *We know that all things work together for good to those who love God.* Chuck Berry was cruising along in his Coupe de Ville and Elvis bumping and grinding and the Beach Boys sang anthems to California, but the basic question in my mind, then and now, is, *What does God want me to do?* I think about this every day. Or I try not to think about it and thus think even harder about it. *Love the Lord thy God with all thy heart and all thy might. And love thy neighbor as thyself.* I sit and ponder this with the trash culture bumping and grinding outside the window and the powerful undertow of narcissism tugging, and I believe I serve God and my neighbor by paying diligent, prayerful, and playful attention to my peculiar gifts, such as they are, and doing good work that supports the weak and lightens up the heavy. I belong to the Church of Work and Prayer. I was young in the time of hippiedom and flittery-skittery tie-dye people in flowing locks with their dreamy yawps about illusion/reality and druggy sitar-ridden music, and they were not from my church. I knew an English major dropout who felt a holy calling to raise sheep and live like a medieval serf in a makeshift yurt while making helpless animals miserable that he had no idea how to herd or care for. Not my church. Coke and speed and marijuana didn't interest me for some reason and we Christians have no need of barbiturates, we are sleepy enough as it is.

My politics doesn't come from the Sixties, it comes from my parents' generation who stepped out of high school into the Depression, hoed corn, drove truck, pumped gas, made do, bopped around on not much dough, went off in 1942 and fought the good war and came home and enjoyed the democratic prosperity of the

Fifties. Satirists portrayed them as anti-intellectuals and raging conformists, but I think they were just happy they had survived so much trouble and danger and had a roof over their heads and food on the table. They were public-spirited, joiners of committees, school board stalwarts, volunteer firemen, softball coaches, scoutmasters, Sunday school teachers, and the women—this was back before it took two people working 60-hour weeks to support a middle-class family—were ferocious do-gooders in the community, the angels of the library, the muscle behind the school bond issue, the church ladies, the surrogate mothers, organizers of festivals, tireless fundraisers. Sometimes satirists are dead wrong. What seemed like conformity was really a low level of narcissism: my parents and their contemporaries believed in a sort of public happiness that found full expression at Anoka High School graduation—the wave of warm buttery emotion at the playing of "Pomp and Circumstance" and the singing of the national anthem, the flashbulbs popping as the children processed in their gowns and mortarboards, the good feelings for teachers and school and community, even if the speaker was a dud and a windbag. The loyalty to the community was palpable. They believed that Anoka, Minnesota, was a uniquely wonderful place and we were all terribly lucky to live there. They bestowed on us a profound sense of well-being. As a teenage satirist, I saw this as complacency. Today, I see it as happiness.

My politics is somehow descended from the kindness of my aunts, apolitical though they appeared to be. My tireless Aunt Elsie kept a lovely home, so clean and fragrant, created perfect Sunday dinners, offered exquisite hospitality, and when Uncle Don felt called to become an itinerant preacher, she went with him—her kindness was portable, her hospitality was not about fine china and napkins. Aunt Ruth was short and round with sweet little chins and when Dad and I dropped in to see her, she hid her ashtray and cigarettes, as if it were a big secret. She was the rebel in his family and so was even more tender and loyal and nostalgic about family. Aunt Josephine was tall and handsome, her black hair tied up, her well-kept garden, and Aunt Bessie the family historian and wit, and Aunt Eleanor who marshaled the big Keillor family Thanksgivings for years, an outdoorswoman who skied and kept horses and cut trees and drove around to check on her elderly neighbors almost up to the day she died, in her kitchen, fixing Thanksgiving dinner. I do not remember these Christian women as judgmental or sarcastic or authoritarian: they were the soul of kindness and their spirit points to the politics that sees to children, the sick, the poor, the wayward, the downcast, and lets the slick and the strong do for themselves.

A health-care system that puts the uninsured through a bureaucratic wringer or schools that force parents to leap tall buildings in order to get special services for kids who need them—my aunts would be shaking their heads.

My ancestors made a bigger impression on me than my contemporaries did. My ancestors told me, in plain Protestant fashion, to Work, Achieve, Be Somebody, Question Authority, Don't Be a Chip on the Tide, Attend to Your Conscience, Be Your Own Man. The easy spiritual transformations of the Sixties and the talk about the system being broken struck me as juvenile, or obtuse: if water flows from the tap and the buses run and the mailman brings the mail and the newspaper lands on your porch in the morning with a fiery editorial against ignorance and corruption, the system is working okay—the rest is up to you. I could appreciate the Christian aspects of hippiedom, the communalism, the embrace of poverty, the love of the land, the tolerance, the cheery potluck suppers and the singing and barefoot dancing, the openheartedness, but the writing was vaporous, elusive. Aiming for universality, it only reached bland. Dip into Allen Ginsberg's big brick of a *Collected Poems* or Bob Dylan's free-association lyrics or Richard Brautigan's whimsy and you get an idea of the hokum that passed for philosophy back then.

My generation went from voodoo Buddhism and the atmospherics of the Grateful Dead (the band for whom no long-playing album could be long enough) to the bourgeois comforts of wine and cheese and extra-virgin olive oil and vintage balsamic vinegar, high-end coffee beans, the search for the ultimate jeans and the latest omniscient book and the deepest massage. They lived most intensely through media, were happy jargonizers, happily self-absorbed. No, my politics comes from my family, who believed in paying your taxes and looking out for people in trouble. The narcissist New Agers became the narcissist Republicans. People with too much money and too little character, all sensibility and no sense, all nostalgia and no history. It's the Republican Party that followed its nose and swung to the right and I am standing where my people stood back when this was one country, before the deluge of delusion.

Chapter 4

ANOKA HIGH SCHOOL

A Bush fellow named Michael Brown
Was busy when New Orleans went down,
Deciding between
The pink and the green
Scarves with his mauve dressing gown.

I AM A CHILD of public education. My parents had six children and there was no choice but to put their trust in the Anoka public schools. They packed me off to Benson School on the day after Labor Day, 1948, with lunch money in a small brown envelope and a tablet and pencils in a pencil box and told me to keep my nose clean and do what the teacher said. Mrs. Shaver was my first-grade teacher, St. Estelle, who noticed I was slow to read and kept me after school to read aloud to her as she corrected papers. She made me feel I was entertaining her, not that I was dumb. I read page after page and when Bill the janitor walked in to sweep up, she said, "Listen to him, Bill. Doesn't he read beautifully?" The old man listened, broom in hand, the boy read aloud, the teacher beamed. I was in remedial reading and I felt like the star of the show. An act of kindness still vivid to me fifty-seven years later, still reverberating in the tunnels of my life.

Parents did not supervise their children's schooling then, just as they didn't manage our social lives—*parenting* wasn't a verb and children didn't have "playdates," we just went out the door and fell into some company or other, a band of robbers, or the Confederate cavalry, or an Ojibway war party, and as for school, Mother looked at the class projects I brought home and commented on the penmanship, and she looked at the report card when Mrs. Shaver sent it home, but teachers were deferred to back then. And so, amazingly, we learned "Frankie and Johnny" in the fourth grade, a traditional ballad about a pimp and a prostitute—unthinkable now—including the lines:

The first time she shot him he staggered.
The second time she shot him he fell.
The third time there was a southwest wind
From the northeast corner of hell.

There we are in the class photograph, Benson School, 1952: the girls in corduroy jumpers and the boys in plaid shirts, our hair slicked down and combed, our clean hands folded on the maple desks, the map of the United States of America hanging in the back of the room. We aren't handsome or stylish children, as children today are, and we didn't bathe every day, just on Saturday night, and in between we washed our faces, no deodorant for us, we smelled like kids, not citrus fruit, but we were terribly anxious to please and most of us, thanks to Mrs. Shaver and Mrs. Moehlenbrock, loved school. I'm in the second row from the left, fifth desk from the front, the boy in steel-rim glasses, the good speller, competing with Billy Pedersen for Champion Reader honors. My mother made sure I had clean clothes, some from the Sears, Roebuck catalog and some handed down from cousins and one pair of jeans from my sister that zipped up the side. Mother reminded me to say "Please" and "Excuse me" and "May I—" (not "Can I—") and to pay attention in school and not daydream. A report card with poor marks in deportment was not taken lightly. We were not going to be scofflaws and scapegraces and illiterate ne'er-do-wells. A mark of Satisfactory in arithmetic indicated a need to reform and do better. It wasn't enough to say you weren't interested in arithmetic. Maybe you weren't but you should pay attention and learn something and not waste the teacher's time.

For seventh grade, I got on the yellow school bus and rode it ten miles north to Anoka where I spent six years in Anoka High School, where my dad had graduated and all my Keillor aunts and uncles. Anoka was a river town, on the Rum and Mississippi, with a bustling Main Street and a Carnegie library and a handsome old redbrick county courthouse with a steeple sitting high and proud in the courthouse square. A quiet town where the front-page news in the Anoka *Herald* tended to be about blood drives and band concerts and SCOUTMASTER PAUL E. WETHERN HONORED FOR 25 YEARS OF SERVICE.

In Anoka High School you found yourself among

farm kids in faded plaid shirts smelling of hay, the hab-
erdasher's kid in his snazzy loafers and yellow cardigan
sweater, the greasers in black slacks and pink shirts,
their customized cars rumbling into the parking lot in
the morning, and the debate team crowd who were
earnest and ambitious and alert, ready to leap in with a
rebuttal, and the student council crowd (clean, well
dressed, anxious to be liked, to have a Nice Personality),
and the brainy kids (gawky, innocent, clueless about social life, biding their time, waiting to migrate to some-
place hospitable), and the fraternity of jocks in their
letter jackets who had to be careful not to appear brainy.
Then there were the oddballs like me, outsiders, starved
for approval, doinking around writing poems or drawing cartoons or doing Bob & Ray comedy routines or
thinking about space travel. We were celibates, unkissed
by anybody, our dignity was too brittle to risk rejection.
I read self-help books, such as we had in 1958, and they
said, "Just be yourself," which did not seem to me a
good idea.

I wasn't very bright but I disguised my ordinariness
by being extremely quiet so some teachers imagined I
was an introspective genius. Others wondered if I were

deaf. A person almost always burnishes his reputation by shutting up: I learned that as a boy. I practiced the art of invisibility, the gift of the middle child in a large family, a sort of vacancy or blankness, and teachers looked right through me and asked the person behind me to come to the blackboard and work out the math problem, and girls looked through me as if I were foliage. I didn't mind.

I was six foot two, 136 pounds with my shoes on. I looked like a folded ironing board with hair. I didn't go around mirrors. I was so nearsighted that without my glasses I lived in an impressionist world, like Monet's. I was in the Young Democrats Club and the girls I knew were Democrats and sympathetic to needy cases. The club took a ski trip to Theodore Wirth Park, my first time on skis. These were the wooden kind with the single leather strap across your shoes. I got in line at the top of the hill. I didn't use poles because I had no idea what to do with them. I pushed off from the top of the hill when nobody was looking and suddenly I was a physics experiment, trying to stay vertical, hands over my head, trees racing by, the law of gravity all over me, and a small spruce zoomed toward me, three feet high, and I leaned to one side and the ground came up and whacked me and I slid on my face for a hundred feet or so and collected a few pounds of snow under my shirt and pants, and hiked down the hill to the ski lodge and there was my crowd, the doinks, the gimps, the good losers, hanging around the lobby fireplace and pretending to have a very, very good time waiting to go home. I took a cup of spiced tea and sat down on the couch and glimpsed myself in an old cracked mirror across the room, a small dark cloud with a lizard face, inept, impoverished, faintly ludicrous, and was grateful finally to go home and climb into a good book.

There were some lovely moments with girls, lounging in swimsuits in a dark green gazebo on a long sloping lawn by the river, and talking and smoking, trying to get the hang of cigarette inhalation, being intellectual, arguing with terrible certainty that the world had taken a fatal turn and was about to end in nuclear conflagration—a dark imagination was a sure way to be taken seriously. I longed to have a girlfriend to whisper affection to in the dark, and neck with, the little ballet of tenderness, the electricity, the delicacy of touch and countertouch. I wondered if something terrible was wrong with me that I hadn't kissed a girl yet—16, 17, 18—when did normal people start doing this? I sent away for a nudist magazine with black-and-white photos of naked people playing volleyball, which I read secretly in the basement and one day, hearing footsteps on the stairs, stuffed it into a bookshelf full of old Sugar Creek Gang and Nancy Drew books and fled, and never found it again. Somebody took it and threw it away, but nothing was said to me about it. We were good at silence in our family.

Altogether the Class of 1960, Anoka High School, formed a picture of democracy that I will carry for the rest of my life. We went through everything together— the embarrassment, walking to the front of Miss Person's speech class and turning and facing the music, or standing in gym shorts and fermented socks in a line of boys waiting to do a flying somersault and thinking to myself, "Someday I won't have to do this," the dull misery of indifferent teachers, a lingering sense of dread about the future, the gathering sense of inevitable failure and disgrace. All of us odd ducks lined up in our graduation gowns and paraded onto the football field that June evening with no idea what life would deal out to us. Not a clue.

But it was there at Anoka High School, that big, bland beige-tiled building, that Mr. Hochstetter encouraged my literary pretensions. He was a brilliant man who paced his classroom declaiming about Twain and Mencken and George Ade and how Luther's Reformation had paved the way for social criticism like Sinclair Lewis's *Main Street* while the boys in the back of the room dozed or read comics. He liked me and said I had talent to write, and a kind word or two is all a boy needs. The heart almost bursts with pleasure. He directed me to the Minneapolis Public Library where I climbed the stairs past the Egyptian mummy in its stone coffin and entered into the stacks and there was pure heaven. I hadn't thought about college, not considering myself slick or bright enough to make a go of it, being from Podunkville, but I was at home in a library, utterly in my element, and the University of Minnesota had an enormous library, so I would give that a try.

Chapter 5

1960

They taught about sex at the Academy,
Genetics, biology, anatomy—
Which I never learned
Because my head was turned
By the girl who sat just ahademy.

IN SEPTEMBER 1960, the night before classes began at the University of Minnesota, I rode a Greyhound north to Isle to pick up a car at my uncle's Ford dealership. Near Milaca, as I sat reading a book—Camus' *The Myth of Sisyphus*, I think—there was a flash of light, I was thrown to my feet, the bus careened off the highway and down in the ditch and up into a cornfield, and stopped. The driver sat stunned and silent at the wheel and some of us charged off the bus into the dark. A line of cars sat on the road. As we made our way there, we saw bodies on the pavement. Two of them, and men bent over them, and the glitter of broken glass, and a station wagon in the opposite ditch, the car our bus had hit head-on, its hood and engine shoved halfway in, and the half-naked body of a young man—dead, somebody said. So were the two in the road, a man and a woman. A fourth man was badly hurt. I stood dumbly on the shoulder, cars inching past me. A few feet away, on the open tailgate of the car, the bare feet of the dead young man lying facedown in the dimness. I imagined the four had spent the weekend at their lake cabin up north and were heading home to Minneapolis. The dad swung out to pass a slower car, passed it, saw the bus headlights, swung back, maybe too fast or too far, lost control. A priest knelt by one of the bodies and put his head down next to the head lying facedown on the asphalt and spoke to it prayerfully. It was a warm night, the smell of field corn in the air and the hushed voices of the scattered onlookers.

A true tragedy, three people killed suddenly—driving toward the city, listening to the radio, talking, smoking, then terror, no time to scream, blinding lights, a pounding heart and death. So why was I so excited, even exhilarated? I was alive, for one thing, and I was 18 and eager for impressions, and I couldn't wait to get to Isle and tell them what I had seen.

*

Two weeks later, John F. Kennedy came to Minneapolis to give a speech in his campaign for president and I went. New haircut, close-cropped, what was called an Ivy League cut, new horn-rim glasses, chinos, white shirt, corduroy jacket with elbow patches, and Pall Malls in my pocket. I sat in the balcony of the auditorium, to Kennedy's right, high above his head, watching him and the crowd enthralled by him, people standing and pressing forward, his hands in his jacket pockets, rocking forward on his toes, the chestnut hair and brilliant grin as he stood doused in applause, glowing in the light, everyone standing and cheering for that fine figure of a man, how he modestly ducked his head and shook hands with the dignitaries on the dais, grinned at the audience, gripped the podium, gave a little wave to the balcony, and the applause went on and on.

Six months before, we Young Democrats of Anoka High School had cheered for our senator, Hubert H.

Humphrey, in his losing battle with Kennedy in the primaries, and some of the idealists felt that Hubert got robbed in West Virginia, that Kennedy's old man had bought the nomination and the machine politicians had him in their pocket. (*Machine* was our term for people who were good at getting out the vote.) My classmate Barbara read somewhere that Kennedy's father was a rum runner during Prohibition and this disturbed her. We sat in our bathing suits on the grass by the beach on the Mississippi, both of us pale, shade seekers, and she poured out her bitterness that Hubert, a true Democrat who fought the good fight for equal rights for Negroes, had been passed over in favor of the son of a crook. It just wasn't right. I didn't understand why anyone who possessed such a fabulous body as hers should be bitter, ever. She wore a one-piece white swimsuit, the top clamped on to her breasts, the bottom she kept tugging down and adjusting. She was such an idealist that I never even held hands with her for fear of offending her. Never considered it. She adored Hubert, who was a legend in Minnesota, an intellectual and yet ebullient, a shining presence at the Aquatennial parade every summer, perched on the back of a white convertible, grinning, waving, always charged up in the presence of a crowd. Everyone got a kick out of seeing Hubert. But he did not travel well. In Minnesota, he seemed almost perfect, a personable and principled man, and on the road he sounded shrill, slightly hysterical compared to Kennedy, who was the coolest politician ever, a handsome war hero with the Irish gift of spontaneous wit. Hubert had a tendency to orate, to rise to a high pitch and then stay there, to reach his climax and keep adding more climaxes, and Kennedy was understated, slightly self-mocking, and charismatic: you couldn't take your eyes off him.

Barbara went east for the summer and I got a summer job as a dishwasher at the Evangeline Hotel for Women on Loring Park in Minneapolis. I wore a Kennedy button on my T-shirt at work, perspiring in my white apron, lugging the trays of steaming hot plates off the conveyer. I scrubbed cooking pots, chipping burnt crust off the bottoms. I peeled potatoes. Dishwashing brings out the romantic in a man. You come out of the steam and heat of the scullery with the smell of detergent in your nose, and the beauty of the world overwhelms you. An ordinary park with grass and trees is like the gardens of Versailles, and by September, when classes started, I was writing big thoughts in my journal. *Death is the admission price we pay at the end of the most wonderful show there is. There are no free tickets. Being fully alive is the only true success; to not love is a form of destruction.* I walked onto campus for the first day of classes, a survivor of a fatal collision, and up the mall to Northrop Auditorium and looked up at its great pillars and the Jeffersonian inscription on the facade above, *Founded in the faith that men are ennobled by understanding, Dedicated to the advancement of learning and the search for truth, Devoted to the instruction of youth and the welfare of the state.* Along the mall, a stately parade of utilitarian brick buildings with pillars pasted to their fronts, a river of humanity flowing under the canopy of majestic elms, lost freshmen lolling on the steps studying campus maps and planning their route from one class to the next, and a procession of Africans and Indians and Pakistanis and Koreans come to study plant agronomy and engineering, Africans blacker than midnight who spoke with British accents like John Gielgud's, black Africans speaking beautiful French (I turned and followed them, eavesdropping, so astonishing this was to hear), bearded Sikhs in turbans, women in saris with red dots painted on their foreheads, Korean War vets in fatigues and GI sunglasses, old bearded lefties in turtlenecks clutching their *I. F. Stone's Weekly* and the *Realist*, cigarette-smoking women playing the role of troubled intellect or Audrey Hepburn heroine, cool people who wore dark glasses, people who might have been poets. Some obvious jocks, crew cuts, jerseys, bowlegged, but few of those compared to the crowd of anxious, bookish people en route to serious encounters with history and literature. Finally, after years of being a bookish outcast, here there were more of us than of them. Ambition everywhere you looked, electric currents of it jazzing the air.

I walked over to Dinkytown to buy my books at Perrine's, down the street from Al's Breakfast Nook, near Vescio's and a rat's nest of a bookstore called Heddon's whose snowy-haired proprietor, after pondering a moment, could reach into the third orange crate from the bottom and pull out the very book you asked for, and Virg 'N' Don's Grocery (whose friendly proprietors seemed to have made that pun accidentally), and a coin laundry called The Tub, and McCosh's Bookstore, the grave bearded McCosh who liked to tack up anarchist aphorisms and pictures of Orwell and Kerouac and Paul Krassner, and the Gray's Drugstore lunch counter (a grilled cheese sandwich, chili, and a vanilla shake, please) and a fine little coffeehouse called the Ten O'Clock Scholar where a beaky kid with brushy hair played a battered guitar and sang "O Fair and Tender Ladies" and *It's dark as a dungeon and damp as the dew, where the dangers are many and the pleasures are few*. The stage was in front, before the big double plate-glass window, and sometimes a passerby stopped on the sidewalk, peered in the window, into the dark room, and then realized the audience was looking at him and fled.

I walked over to Folwell Hall, home of the English Department and the divine Miss Sarah Youngblood and craggy old Huntington Brown and stammering Samuel Monk and Toni McNaron who propounded Milton and Archibald Leyasmeyer the Chaucerian and other noble and learned friends of literature, and I felt grateful that this institution had opened its doors to a dreamer like me who had no clear vocation whatsoever. I was operating on a wistful urge to sit in libraries and be a writer. That was all. No idea of how to do it, who to talk to, where to go. Admiration for the *New Yorker*, of course, and a vague hope that talent will rise to the surface, but no clear idea that I might be one of the risers. Ambitious boys were climbing the slopes toward law school, smart girls in chemistry lab were marching toward distinction in medicine, others plotting their course toward the Foreign Service or academia or the ag business. Myself, I just hoped to get lucky.

I paid $71 for a quarter's tuition and another $10 or so for my books, a political science text, a volume of Horace and a Latin dictionary, and Strunk and White's *Elements of Style* for my composition course—and notebooks with the university seal on the cover (*Omnibus Artibus, Commune Vinculum*) and I went and took a seat in the long reading room in Walter Library. Around me, men and women bent to the hard work of scholarship, folks for whom attending college was not an assumed privilege. The vets on the GI Bill and the African and Asian exchange students and all the ones who were the first in their family to attend college, whose parents' own hopes had been deferred by the Depression and the war—these students approached the U with a great chins-up, pencils-sharpened sense of purpose. They sat at the long oak library tables, heads bowed, rows and rows of them, reading, reading, reading—sons of garage mechanics on their way to medical school, daughters of dairy farmers out to become professors of Romance languages—a great American migration as inspiring as anything that took place on the Oregon Trail. These pioneers craved a life in which beauty and delight and intellectual challenge are staples; they wanted to travel, read novels, go to the theater, be smart about the world and not reflexively pessimistic like their parents, have far-flung experiences. The craving for experiences was powerful. Love and adventure and interesting work—a great many of us, dreading the regimentation of corporate life, would head for the burgeoning nonprofit world. Such a purposeful bunch—who looked like me and had no money either—who plowed through the texts and took notes and shushed up the goofballs in their midst. Boys and girls who came to the library to goof off were glared at and told to be still—this never happened in high school! These were people with a sense of vocation. It was a Thomas Hart Benton mural come to life—"The Children of the Great Plains Claiming Their Birthright."

Their once-in-a-lifetime chance to realize their God-given talent, as medical technicians or scholars of medieval painting or the operas of Verdi or the breeding rituals of the Arctic ptarmigan. No guarantee of success, or even of gainful employment. Pure free enterprise.

Dad had made it clear that he couldn't pay for my education, which I hadn't asked him to, and I was relieved not to have to consider an offer. A nice clean break. I got a job working the 6–10 A.M. shift in the big parking lot on the river flats for $1.48 an hour. Nine hundred cars, and it filled up by 7:30 so there you were with a couple of hours of paid study time. You learned to ignore your fellow parking lot attendant who liked to tell about students he had seen having sex in parked cars and you applied yourself to the U.S. Constitution and the separation of powers.

I got another job at the student radio station, WMMR, in October, and a tall good-looking guy named Barry Halper showed me how to piece together a newscast from the Associated Press Teletype. They needed someone to do the 12:15 newscast. "Today?" I said. "Today," he said. He showed me how to switch on the microphone, read the VU meter, adjust the headphone volume, showed me the cough switch, and an hour later I sat down in a tiny room with green acoustic-tile walls at a table covered with green felt and switched on the mike and a red bulb lit up and I read the news under a gooseneck lamp, one eye on the big clock on the wall in front of my face. I was nervous of course, but it was a delicious nervousness, an elevation of the senses. I felt sequestered, safe in the studio, a little fortress. I did the newscast and said, "That's the news, reported by Garrison Keillor. This is WMMR, from studios in Coffman Memorial Union, broadcasting at 730 kilocycles." And pressed a button and the tape deck clunked and a recorded voice talked about Campus Pizza and I got up and the next announcer slipped in and played something by Johnny Mathis and I walked out to the hall and Barry Halper nodded at me. "That was not bad," he said.

Barry told me I ought to go cover Kennedy's speech and I rode over to the Minneapolis Auditorium on a chartered bus that was packed, girls sitting on laps, boys crushed together in the aisle. I crushed myself into them and stood pressed against a girl's back, a solid mass of people swaying on the turns. I joined the crush streaming into the hall and climbed up under the rafters as the mighty Wurlitzer played "Happy Days Are Here Again" and sat through the prelims, all the little frogs getting their moment in the sun, and Senator Eugene McCarthy was introduced and then Hubert, who got a long ovation but not too long, and then Orville Freeman got behind the lectern and introduced John F. Kennedy and out he came, covered in glory, and the place almost came loose from its moorings. In that shining moment, standing, grinning amid the tumult, the whistles and the cheers, he truly seemed to rise to meet our hopes for him. I sort of knew the rap against him—he had dodged the issue of McCarthyism; his father's shady fortune had bought the nomination; the grandma of the Democratic Party, Eleanor Roosevelt, couldn't warm up to him because he wasn't Adlai Stevenson—but there in the flesh, he was thrilling; he was the first politician with movie hero presence and he had the elegant dignity of someone who has always known who he is, unlike the herky-jerky Nixon who tried too hard to impersonate himself. Kennedy was classy, not overeager like so many politicians, who were tuned a half step sharp and didn't know how to play the crowd. They could do earnest and hortatory with the three obligatory jokes at the beginning and some keening and baying at the end and the hands-high touchdown pose, but he had more keys on his piano. He had black keys and they didn't. There was playfulness in him; he didn't just preach about freedom, he actually seemed to enjoy it. He was not one of the old jowly guys who peered at TV cameras as if they were booby-trapped and read woodenly from prepared texts and struck the old ritual poses. Kennedy was an improviser. He stood there and grinned and soaked up the applause and then joked about Ted Williams having announced his retirement from the Red Sox at the age of 42—Kennedy was 43—"It shows that perhaps experience isn't enough." Huge laugh—and he tipped his hat to Hubert as a worthy opponent (more applause) and went on to his speech. I remember he quoted Dante—politicians didn't quote Dante then, any more than they'd pose in a little black beret with a cigarette dangling from their lower lip. Kennedy made you believe that at one time in his life he'd sat down and read the *Inferno,* that he lived in a house with books on the shelves and didn't care who knew it, that he might have enjoyed Italy and cared about more than politics. He shared our disdain for the dull-witted bullies of the world who lord it over the meek and lowly. I didn't care that he was rich and Catholic. So what? It felt as if a great loosening was coming and a jazzier spirit was in the air. And we'd have a president for whom we felt admiration. So I became a Democrat. Republicans were those fraternity boys on University Avenue engaged in the manly pursuit of drunkenness and lighting farts, sponsoring the annual Pajama Parade and the Tunic Twirl, singing their raccoon songs, a bunch of glad-handers and blowhards who devoted more attention to their hair than to what lay beneath it.

I walked back to campus from his speech. At 18, I was deeply into my family's history and I felt a connection between Kennedy and my family's New England roots, which I was just then hugely proud of, having recently learned about them. The reference to Dante was, "We have all made mistakes. But Dante tells us that divine justice weighs the sins of the cold-blooded and the sins of the warmhearted on different scales. Better the occasional faults of a party living in the spirit of charity than the consistent omissions of a party frozen in the ice of its own indifference." To me this spoke volumes about the cold legalism of fundamentalist Christianity, which was its dark side—the bright side was the evangelical spirit and the gospel of Jesus Christ who came to free us from bondage—but then there was the cold literalist judgmental schismatic side and the gimlet-eyed blue-nosed martinets who would expel you into outer darkness if you so much as dared to ask questions. My New England ancestors were warmhearted. Joseph Crandall was an associate of Roger Williams who founded the first Baptist church in America in Providence in 1639. Roger Williams had grown up in England when Puritans were burned at the stake and came to Massachusetts Bay Colony where he found the Puritans to be as intolerant as the people who had incinerated them back in England. He founded Rhode Island as a haven for people of all beliefs, including Indians. Roger Williams made Indian languages the great scholarly enterprise of his life. And my ancestor was there with him. And then there was Prudence Crandall who opened a school for young women in Canterbury, Connecticut, in 1831. When she admitted a colored girl the following year, all of the decent white families pulled their children out, whereupon Prudence opened a school for young colored women, the first in the country, which was shut down

by a mob. She was a Quaker. She married a Baptist cler-
gyman named Calvin Philleo and they moved to Kansas
and she kept on teaching and was a staunch advocate of
equal rights for women until she died in 1890. Mark
Twain once spoke admiringly of Prudence Crandall and
I was as proud of her as I could be, my ancestor who
stood up to a mob for what she knew to be right.

In the Great American Divide between the cold
avengers and the sons of liberty, the paranoid and the
happy entrepreneurs, the bullies and the defenders of
justice, Kennedy was over on the side of the warmhearted, and that was his mystique, no mystery about it.

I remember I walked in silence across that high narrow
bridge over the Mississippi gorge and up the empty street
behind Walter Library and thought about Kennedy and
the Crandalls and the University and my ambitions to
be a writer, which seemed to be all tangled up together
in a ball, and I was overjoyed a few weeks later when he
beat Nixon. And then his heroic inauguration, his good
speech with some ringing phrases in it, and the heroic
performance by Robert Frost of "The Gift Outright"—
what a good country to be able to sense the difference
between Nixon and Kennedy, even by a narrow margin.

He stood in the light and he was worthy of our ideals. I never met him or his wife or children. I never was fascinated by their Kennedyness, only by him as president. Under his sway, I signed up for the Don Fraser for Congress campaign in 1962, which knocked off a crusty old Republican in Minneapolis and was managed by Don's wife, Arvonne, a short peppery woman who personified for me the Democratic-Farmer-Labor Party, open-hearted, perpetually hopeful, honest to a fault, and capable of outrage. I was in Eddy Hall on November 22, 1963, when I heard the president had been shot. I was an announcer at the University AM radio station, KUOM, and was sitting in the record library when the secretary, Bobbie, came in and told me. I walked to the United Press Teletype in the hall closet and saw the first fragmentary bulletins, all caps, DALLAS, NOV. 22 (UPI)— THREE SHOTS WERE FIRED AT PRESIDENT KENNEDY'S MOTORCADE IN DOWNTOWN DALLAS—I stood reading this in stunned silence, the Teletype clacking away, and there was something about the president's limp body being carried from the car, and the word *fatally* appeared, and I took the paper into the studio where an actor was reading Tolkien's *The Hobbit* on a show called

Your Novel—he glanced up in alarm and I handed him the bulletin and he said, in a rather grand voice, "I have just been handed a news bulletin"—and I went back to the record library and got a record of, I think, a Spanish Mass and we played the Benedictus. And then Tchaikovsky's *Pathétique.* There was no need for us to read more news, everybody knew the news. Who killed him was never clear and either you read the conspiracy literature or you did not. I didn't. I never could bring myself to visit the assassination museum at the schoolbook depository in Dallas. Nothing I read later about Kennedy and his life essentially changed how I felt about him the night I walked back to campus from his speech in October 1960.

One day in the Scholar coffeehouse, a kid strummed a 12-string guitar and everyone sang, without prompting, *Deep in my heart, I do believe that we shall overcome someday.* With all our hearts. Underneath the thin patina of coolness, we were all church kids. We'd read the prophets, heard the gospel, were exalted by the thought of being soldiers for the Lord and setting the prisoners free. Kennedy didn't live to see it, but it was done in his spirit.

A couple of years after he died, the Mississippi River rose in the spring and there were urgent flood warnings on the radio. One afternoon I put on warm clothes and took the bus to St. Paul and crossed the Wabasha Bridge to the West Side where people were at work filling sandbags and building dikes to save the low-lying houses. It was foggy, and then it began to rain. An army of hundreds of volunteers hard at work, men and women, drawn up in assembly lines, holding the sacks and filling them and passing them in a chain to the dike. It got dark. Nobody left. The Red Cross brought around sandwiches and coffee. We rested and went back to work. Trucks brought in more sand and bags. A couple of front loaders worked at anchoring the dikes with earthen banks. It felt like wartime. I worked until after midnight and lay down in the back of a truck under a tarp and slept until daybreak and got up stiff and cold and they brought us more sandwiches and coffee and I got back in the gang and worked until noon. Someone said the flood would crest that evening. Someone worried about the dike bursting. A man said, "When they go, they go slow, they don't go sudden." I wasn't sure about that, but I stayed because everyone else stayed. I sort of collapsed in the afternoon and was going to go home but slept a couple of hours on a tarp in somebody's front yard, and when I woke up, there was water in the street, people wading through it, some men with muddy overalls, pitched emotion in the air, though nobody said much. We had put so much into beating back the flood, and we kept working—shovel, fill, tie, and pass, shovel, fill, tie, and pass—and felt privileged to be there doing it. I could hear the river boiling by and slabs of ice heaved up on the dike and National Guardsmen patrolling, and when people couldn't stand up any longer, they sat down and ate baloney sandwiches and drank coffee. And got back up.

I went home in the morning. It was so overwhelming, I sat on the bed and cried. For the relief of getting out of those mud-crusted clothes and standing under a hot shower, but also for what I'd seen, the spirit of all those workers caught up in the job of saving their neighbors' houses. Forget all the political jabber and gossip, all the theoretical balderdash and horsefeathers, here is reality: the river rises up in its power and majesty, and the people rise up in theirs, and while one can do only so much, you must do that much, and we did. None of the news reports captured the reality of that event, which was the spirit of the crowd, of which I was one. An experience that warms a Democrat's heart, a scene from *Grapes of Wrath*, or the crossing of the Red Sea. The People, yes.

By God, no matter what Republicans say, the people of this country really do care about each other. We are not a cold people. By God, when John F. Kennedy said, "Ask what you can do for your country," he spoke to this country's heart and conscience. My teachers Miss Story, Miss Melby, Mrs. Fleischman, Mr. Faust, Mr. Hochstetter, Miss Hattendorf: those tireless encouragers and inspirers. Children of the Depression, they were impelled toward public service, a good career. For them teaching was a shining ideal and also the path out of a hard life on the farm, a life they knew too well, the life of serfs. The very word *education* was dazzling to them. The life of the mind is beautiful to those who have done laundry by hand and hoed corn and hauled water for the baths. Miss Hattendorf grew up on a farm in Iowa; her German parents sent her and her sisters to board with a family in town so they could attend high school. When Miss Hattendorf was about to leave for the University of Chicago and it came time to say good-bye and get in the car and go to the train, she looked at her mother standing at the kitchen sink—"I wanted to hug her, but I couldn't do it. She was a stranger to me. They wanted me and my sisters to get a good education and they made big sacrifices and that was one of them: they didn't know us anymore and we didn't know them."

There are many stories of sacrifice and idealism like hers—and one of the dark deeds of Republicans is their denigration of public service and their characterization of public servants as parasites, busybodies, incompetents. To the crook, everyone is a crook; and to Republicans, the idea of serving the public good is counterfeit on the face of it—they never felt such an urge, therefore it must not exist. But John F. Kennedy knew it and gave voice to it. My teachers felt it every day.

Chapter 6

❋ ○○○○○○○○ ☼ ○○○○○○○○ ❋

THE SPIRIT OF EQUALITY

As a youth, our president, George,
Spent summer nights on the front porch,
Giving wedgies and hickeys
And drinking gin rickeys
And lighting his farts with a torch.

JOHN F. KENNEDY made a big impression on me, but attending the University was what confirmed me as a Democrat, the thought that the taxpayers of Minnesota really had faith that knowledge and understanding ennoble us. An egalitarian spirit prevailed at the U. There was no rank, no hazing, no freshman beanies, we were all in the same boat. You were Mr. Keillor to your professor and he was Mr. Brown to you. You looked him in the eye. You said, "I don't get this" and he explained it

93

to you. That was his job. Yours was to pay attention. Money was no social asset whatsoever and if you went around in expensive clothes you were regarded with pity or scorn. A few goofball freshmen showed up in brand-new suits for fall classes and they stood out in the crowd as if they wore red rubber noses and fright wigs. Everybody from the president to the deans and the faculty had their home addresses and phone numbers listed in the University directory, and if you were brave enough, you could ring up Dean McDiarmid or Vice President Willey and tell him your troubles. I did not but the phone numbers were there and I suppose somebody did. On my slender parking lot wages I was able to buy a season ticket to the concerts in Northrup and I saw Isaac Stern, Arthur Rubinstein, Andrés Segovia, the Royal Danish Ballet doing a Balanchine program, the great Swedish tenor Jussi Bjöerling, the Cleveland Orchestra, Glenn Gould—you could get a balcony seat for $1.50, about an hour's wage. I couldn't afford to see the Metropolitan Opera on their annual tour but one evening I did look up at a window on the side of Northrup and see a tall slender dark-haired woman standing naked in front of a full-length mirror for a whole minute, studying herself. A wardrobe lady sat nearby, smoking, reading a newspaper. The dark-haired woman turned, facing me, hands on hips, one leg extended, looking over her shoulder at her rump, her delicate bush and maroon nipples, like a painting—*Nude Dancer Before a Mirror*.

Robert Frost came to campus one fall and drew a capacity crowd of 5,000 at Northrup Auditorium, the great stooped white-maned old bear reciting by heart "Stopping by Woods on a Snowy Evening" and the crowd hushed in the cathedral of poetry—"For Once, Then, Something" and "The Oven Bird" and "Fire and Ice" and the one about the lover's quarrel with the world—that soft lyrical cranky uncle voice beloved since junior high, a godlike presence in our midst, and afterward a hundred of us acolytes gathered at the back door to view the great man up close. I was proud of him for drawing that huge crowd and performing so well. He eased his old body down the stairs, our grand paterfamilias, and mingled with us, chatted, answered a few questions—I remember clearly, nobody asked for his autograph—and then he climbed into a black Chrysler and was taken off to lunch with the faculty. But we students were as important as anybody else and weren't held behind ropes or shushed. That was how it was at the U. The field was wide open. At the *Minnesota Daily* and its literary arm, the *Ivory Tower,* you submitted your stuff and back came a polite note, "Sorry," and that week they printed George Amabile's poems instead of yours, but you sent more and of that second batch the editor accepted two and the next month they appeared, big glutinous symbolist things about owls on moonless nights flying to Arabia, all in lowercase, and you snatched ten copies out of a paper box and took them home to save to show your grandchildren you once were a writer. The publications weren't in the grip of a gang, they were open to walk-ons.

College. The only time in your life when you can be gloriously, ridiculously full of yourself and get away with it. A luxury once reserved for the aristocracy, now extended to the children of postal workers. I grew a beard. I wore a fringed leather vest, sometimes beads. I tried cigars, a pipe. I wanted to be Norman Mailer. I was a middle-class kid from the West River Road where late at night fireflies sparkled in the field behind the dark houses with blue TV light flickering and the rich green moist lawns and the great harmonic of lawn and white houses and black asphalt and ten miles south on the Mississippi I found the University where I could imagine a larger life and hope to escape the downdraft of the suburbs and do what I loved to do, write, though it seemed presumptuous. I imagined getting published in the *New Yorker*. I hung around the *Daily* offices, free of the petty miseries of high school. Jocks no longer mattered so much. The bullies had dispersed, the cliques of town girls, too. The University was freedom. A friend of mine dropped out sophomore year and married his girlfriend and they bought a little yellow rambler in Coon Rapids, the down payment a gift from her parents. He was a warehouse clerk and his wife got pregnant and woke up in a foul mood every morning and he went off to eight hours of an automaton job. What a waste of a perfectly good life. Women were the great tamers; they took you in hand and trained you to accept the leaden social life and waxen solemnity of suburbia and instead of bumming around Europe you'd be spending a week with her parents in a Florida condo. Women put their arms around you and cried that they loved you and wanted to make you happy and *bwanngggg* a trapdoor popped open and you slid down the chute into a job you despised and a frazzled marriage in a crackerjack house with a mountain of a mortgage. I intended to escape that. I longed for my flesh to touch someone else's but I remained chaste. I sat in clouds of cigarette smoke in a classroom smelling of linseed-oiled floors and listened to James Wright lecture on Dickens and gazed at the lovely girls in horn-rim glasses. I liked strolling around campus at night with Gail who wrote for the paper or my classmate Mary, put my arm around her waist and hooked my little finger in her belt loop and she with her arm around the back of me, hooked together, talking about life's persistent questions, arms riding across each other's butts, our hips moving in meter, which, we two being different heights, came out in 9/7 time, like an old Swedish step dance, and I would maybe recite Housman's poem about being 20—"And take from seventy springs a score, / It only leaves me fifty more. / And since to look at things in bloom / Fifty springs are little room, / About the woodlands I will go / To see the cherry hung with snow"—and wind up back at Murphy Hall and the *Daily* office.

For winter quarter, I got the 5 A.M. shift at a ten-acre

gravel parking lot on the West Bank, overlooking the Mississippi. I was turning into a night owl, always up past midnight, and the alarm clock went off at 4:00 and I lay in the warm trench of my bed, reviewing my options, preferring sleep, longed for it, nodded off, which shocked me into wakefulness and I rolled out and drove to town through the snowy world and parked beside the parking lot shack and hiked to the far end of the lot, flashlight in hand, like a sheep shearer waiting for the herd to come piling through the gate. The lot sloped down to the edge of the bluff and I looked down on Bohemian Flats, a ragtag village on the riverbank. Old frame houses that got flooded out every spring, where old Swedes and bohunks lived a subsistence life in the middle of the Twin Cities. Smoke rose from their chimneys. One of the other parking attendants said there was a whorehouse down there. "Ten bucks a shot," he said. "Indian women." I got good at parking. The cars came in a rush, starting at 6:30. Three ticket sellers stood in the street, and the flagman stood at the top of the lot and directed the flow to where I was conducting them into their spots, straight lines, double rows. No painted lines on the gravel, I did it all by eye.

I had to direct each car with strong hand signals into its correct space, the Otto Klemperer of the automobile, and discourage the tendency to freelance and veer off toward a more convenient place. Every morning there were three or four pioneers who wanted to start their own rows. You had to yell to the flagman to hold the traffic and then you ran over toward the miscreant's car and yelled, "Your car will be towed in ten minutes." The mention of towing got their attention, but you had to make it sound real. "That's a $25 fine." Usually that was enough to get them to move the car. If they hesitated, I said, "Plus $25 for the impound lot. It's up to you." I had no idea who to call to come tow a car or what they would say, I just did what other attendants said to do, and it worked. Creative parking couldn't be allowed, chaos would result, cars skewed everywhere, blocking other cars, holding up traffic, people late, angry, honking— it was my responsibility to make the grid system work. For the common good. To be direct. Exercise authority. *No, sir. Not there. Over here. Right here. Yes. Here.* Your individualists and comedians would test the limits, and if you gave them an inch, anarchy would ensue, cars going every which way like confused buffalo. Be firm. Make that bozo back up six inches. *Straighten that line. Thank you.* If you accept variance, the line will buckle. If you do your job right, the lot fills to capacity in half an hour, you put up the full sign and huddle in the shack, the electric heater blazing away, and you take up with Natasha and Prince Andrei and *War and Peace* for Mr. Milgrom's Humanities class until 9 A.M. when the shift ends and you leg it over the Washington Avenue bridge to the East Bank. A cup of vending machine coffee and a Baby Ruth and off to class.

In the winter, we packed into Williams Arena to cheer the hockey team against our deadly rival, the Fighting Sioux of North Dakota. Blood lust in the air. Our Gophers were all Minnesota boys and the Sioux were all Canucks, paid thugs, big bruisers, mercenaries, and when a Sioux got ridden into the boards, we cheered from the bottom of our hearts. I dated a quiet girl, a church organist, and at hockey games she screeched and booed like a true peasant. I wrote a poem about hockey and took it to a writers' club meeting at Professor Hage's house and the poet James Wright said something encouraging about it and my face burned with pleasure. I can still picture it in my mind, where I was sitting, where he sat, and feel my face getting warm.

The University was a monument to the Jeffersonian faith in the power of learning and in the ability of all people to recognize and embrace excellence, a grand old American notion. To offer Jussi Bjöerling and Arthur Rubinstein to 18-year-old kids at prices they can afford is an astonishment. Utterly. To attend such artistry can change a person's life. But that was the spirit of the Morrill Act of 1862 that granted to the states a tract of land in proportion to their population for the endowment of a state university to teach the classic curriculum as well as courses relating to agriculture and industry, open to qualified students regardless of financial means. I paid $71 tuition for a quarter at the U, and today, U of M students pay about $6,000 for a year's tuition, which is $2,000 for what cost me $71, which says a lot about politics today. Tuition has been cranked up as the classic curriculum is doinked around with, language requirements are relaxed and in place of French or German you can take a course in pop culture, thus the idea of excellence is abandoned, a heartless way to welcome the next generation, to sell them a junk car for ten times the money.

My Latin teacher, Margaret Forbes, was an auntly woman, cheery and kind, who ran us through daily translations and sniped at us with questions about the anticipatory subjunctive—subjunctive denotes an act that is expected, *Expectabum dum frater redirect*, I was waiting for my brother to return. And we responded to her *aequo animo*, without anxiety, as she lay open the folded language—*patefacio, patefacere, patefeci, patefactum. O pace in perpetuum*, Margaret, *felicitas aeternas*! Richard Cody taught composition, a slender Englishman sitting at a table on a raised platform, lecturing drily on the art of the essay, which he described as a 440-yard dash through natural obstacles, over rough terrain, an intellectual exercise also meant to be esthetically elegant. We were Minnesota kids striving to imitate William Hazlitt, Joseph Addison, George Orwell, E. B. White, and Norman Mailer. Once Mr. Cody called on me to come forward and read the first page of my essay on manure spreading, one of my jobs on Uncle Jim's farm—a humorous essay, supposedly—and I jumped up to do it and fainted dead away, fell across a row of empty chairs and crashed to the floor and lay there. "Are you all right?" a girl asked under her breath. I got up and Mr. Cody called on someone else. We were all pretty cool back then. Asher Christiansen taught American Government, an elegant little man in dark slacks and gray blazer, bushy eyebrows, mustache, smoking his pipe—half the class smoked too, and I came to associate intellectual seriousness with bad air—propounding his grand theme, that the Constitution was a natural force for civilization, its checks and balances serving to dampen the fires of inner-directed ideologues and bring them into a respectful relationship to their antagonists and attend to the serious business of government. After class, some students formed another smaller class that followed Professor Christiansen out the door and stood in the alley behind Nicholson Hall for a few minutes, a gaggle of fifteen or twenty that dwindled as he headed down the Mall to his office in Ford Hall, arriving there with four or five of us still hanging on. I was a student in the last class he taught. In January I saw the front-page story in the *Daily*: Professor Christiansen had felt ill during lunch at the faculty club and went to a quiet room to lie down and died there of a heart attack. The story said he grew up in Little Falls, graduated from the U, where he taught from 1936 on, with guest stints in Wales, Germany, and Argentina, where he lectured in Spanish. He was 57 years old, married, no children. Just his students.

I stuck around at WMMR and did the noon newscast for six months, five days a week, and then in May was told that the station had been off the air for at least that long. Doggone it. Our engineer, a brilliant young man, had been busy building a state-of-the-art control room and had left transmitter maintenance to others and it had burned out. I was in some anguish over having spent six months editing a newscast so I could sit in a room and read it to myself, but as Barry Halper said, "It was good experience." And had I ever, in those six months, thought about the listeners and wondered why the cards and letters weren't pouring in or trickling in or even dripping in? No. I was having too much fun. "You sound terrific," said Barry. "You could get a job on any station in town." He was a pal and a real positive guy. He was 20, he drove a big white convertible; he was handsome and Jewish and smart; he'd been to LA and

Las Vegas and met Jack Benny and Shelley Berman. If he'd asked me to, I would've shined his shoes.

I was a serious young man and did not go to parties at the U except one in the spring of my sophomore year at somebody's parents' house in Kenwood, a tony neighborhood in Minneapolis, where a mob of students was drinking something called Purple Death out of a washtub in the kitchen. Fortified with this, people started spouting off their big opinions about Kennedy and Hemingway and Ornette Coleman and some of us got into a contest to see who knew more dirty limericks. There was the one about the young man from Buckingham and the young man from St. Paul whose cock was exceedingly small and the Bishop of Chichester and the sailor named Tex who avoided premarital sex and the young woman of Edina and her vagina.

The base of Purple Death was grape Kool-Aid, plus whatever the guests had brought. It was a potluck cocktail: Old Buzzard Breath bourbon, crème de banana, licorice schnapps, vodka, anything would do, and after drinking for a while and telling dirty jokes, some of us headed over to Cedar Lake to go skinny-dipping, and we stripped off our clothes, but it wasn't the erotic thrill it should've been, not for me anyway: I could feel the hangover mounting up behind my forehead, a truly monumental one, with shades of surrealism—I remember naked women and I also remember the dark angel of projectile vomiting—and in the morning I awoke with a taste of what mental illness might be like, a sort of vacancy with dark shadows. And I was glad to be alone.

As U of M students we walked around with a fine chip on our shoulder toward eastern finishing schools like Yale and Harvard where children of privilege slept until noon after a night of inebriation, were brought cucumber sandwiches by a porter, sashayed off to their 3 P.M. music appreciation class, and then played squash until dinner. Oxford and Cambridge were held in even greater contempt: dandruffy men quivering with borrowed sensibility, drinking sherry and propounding fabulous foolishness with great certainty. You walk around with a brown bag lunch and a few bucks in your pocket, trying to scrape together next quarter's tuition, and a little class resentment is good for you, a balm and a prod both. I envied cool people, good tennis players, opera singers, sandy-haired rich guys who looked princely even in ratty old clothes, all Frenchmen, men with lovely girlfriends, guitarists, but the U was the antidote to envy. So many cool people seem on closer examination to be trapped in a set of mannerisms that are not so interesting and lead nowhere, whereas the U appealed to your curiosity and drew you into scholarship, which took you through doors you hadn't known existed. In one smoky classroom after another, sitting elbow to elbow at little arm desks, you felt illuminated: there was a quickening almost like drunkenness, a feeling that you and the professor were adventuring through the drowsy world, privy to great secrets, grasping the outlines of the great continents. I learned how to plant myself in a library chair and open the books and take notes on a yellow legal pad. Having a good ear for multiple-choice tests had gotten me through high school (the correct answer, two-thirds of the time, was C) but now I had to actually do the work. I soldiered through and learned how to write profoundly at great speed late at night about books I barely understood.

American universities have seen radicals and revolutionaries come and go over the years, and all of them put together were not nearly so revolutionary as a land-grant university itself on an ordinary weekday. To give

people with little money a chance to get the best education there is—that is true revolution. When I graduated
from Anoka High School, I believed that my chances
would be as good as anybody else's, and the good people
of Minnesota did not let me down. I got my chance and
right there is where a Democrat is made. A kid from
Anoka sits in a parking lot shack on Fourth Street SE
where, earning $1.48 an hour, he translates Horace for
Mrs. Forbes—whose standards are high—as birds sit
scritching on the telephone wire and a fly buzzes at the
window. A bright fall day and he has no money to speak
of and no clear plan for the future but he has teachers
who engage him with gravity and fervor and that's
enough. That was the true spirit of the University, the
spirit of professors devoted to their work. That was the
heart and soul of the place, not the athletic teams, not
the architecture. The University was Mary Malcolm, a
native of Worthington, who studied in Paris with Nadia
Boulanger and came back to teach music theory for
forty-three years. She had perfect pitch and could write
down on paper anything you could hum or plunk on the
piano. It was Izaak M. Kolthoff, a Dutch chemist who
guided Jewish scientists out of Germany in the Thirties

and worked on the crucial war project of creating synthetic rubber and became a peacenik in the Fifties. It was Marcia Edwards, a chain-smoking authority on adolescent psychology and a fanatical Gopher sports fan who went to angelic lengths to help her students, even lending them money, and who turned down the offer to become dean of the College of Education because she didn't want the hassle, especially the foofaraw of being the first woman dean. It was Bill Marchand who taught Shakespeare to kids majoring in animal husbandry and horticulture. It was Nils Hasselmo who came from Sweden to study the Swedish immigrants and got his doctorate and became president of the U. And it was Margaret Forbes who could make you feel that a few lines of Horace held the key to a nobility available to us all. And if you start to feel ennobled, you lose interest in how you are perceived by other people. You walk into the library and that Niagara of scholarship holds you in your place, the deluge of learning, and you begin to see where work and play become one. And imagine working at something you love. And that was how the University of Minnesota gave me my life.

Chapter 7

REAL LIVES, REAL CONSEQUENCES

So frigid is the harpy Ann Coulter
Icicles hang from her shoulder
And the buzzards shiver
As they peck out her liver
Where she lies naked chained to a boulder.

WE DEMOCRATS are deeply flawed people, but we do stick to our guns, and believe in respect for the individual and public spiritedness and have refused to hitch our wagon to yahooism and intolerance and have supported government as a necessary force for good to "establish justice, ensure domestic tranquility, provide for the common defense, promote the general welfare, and secure the blessings of liberty . . ."

We can be perfectly and sweetly corrupt—I think

back to the logrolling I witnessed at the National Endowment for the Arts, petty politics at work to bestow
public largesse on the projects of one's pals—and Lord
knows we can be earnestly boring. We sermonize about
the Unmet Needs of the dyslexic lesbian and the emo-
tionally disadvantaged Estrogen-American and we prom-
ise the moon on a string and it bores the eyeballs right
out of people. We can be awfully righteous about moral
issues in faraway places: we tend to see more clearly at
a distance and to love humanity in the abstract and forget about the folks across the alley. We take perverse
pleasure in seeing tycoons in handcuffs. We enjoy the
banality of the Trumps and the Bushes and the Hiltons,
their proud illiteracy, their air-conditioned nightmare.
We can take a good high-school course like World Ge-
ography and change it to Frameworks of Belonging and,
instead of teaching kids where Switzerland is, have
them write about feeling lost and disconnected. We can
be weenies, masters of rinky-dink. We can stand up and
argue that *dyslexic* is a marginalizing term and *para-
lexic* is better, that wrong answers are not wrong, but
rather alternative views of the world. We tend to be re-
visionists and dissenters and boycotters and quick to

resign in protest. (The Democrat was shipwrecked on a desert island for years and lived there alone and finally he was rescued and he showed the rescue party around the island. He said, "See there, I built myself a house over there. And over there is my barn. And that building over there is my church." And the rescue party said, "And what's that building back there?" "Oh," he said. "That. That's the church I used to go to.") We took some wrong turns in the past when we swung away from the bread-and-butter AFL-CIO issues and into symbolic stuff like the ERA. We are profoundly indecisive, nervous about strong emotion, reluctant to invoke the Deity, susceptible to the vapors like a herd of turkeys liable to panic at lightning and stampede into a fence and pile up and suffocate. We are capable of doing dumb things in the name of the common good and sponsoring National Self-Awareness Week and printing up brochures reminding people not to walk into open manholes. We have a weakness for rule making to ensure that nothing bad can happen, which leads us into thickets that go nowhere anybody needs to go. A world that is perfectly safe from sexual harassment is a world without flirtation. A world with airtight protection against thieves will have no entrepreneurs. And a world without fiction would be unbearable for all of us. Once, at a party in St. Paul, I heard a woman talk at some length about diversity and how "persons of noncolor" should not impose their majority culture on others, and the phrase "persons of noncolor"—the idea of being colorless—made me reach for my coat and hat. Good-bye, I'm out of here. Call me when you get over it.

We Democrats are at our worst when we lose touch with our principles—the protection of the powerless, paying attention to real consequences in the lives of real people, and not flying on slogans or glib phrases—and when we try to emulate Republicans as we did in signing onto the "war" on drugs that has ruined so many young lives. In our nation's capital, nearly 50% of black men between 18 and 35 are either in prison or on probation or parole—nationally, it's a human disaster: 6.6 million Americans in prison, nearly half of whom are black men. The cruelty of the Sentencing Reform Act of 1984 is stark indeed, and of sentencing guidelines that impose mandatory minimum sentences for minor drug possession—guidelines in the 1986 Anti–Drug Abuse Act that sailed through Congress without benefit of public hearings, drafted before an election by Democrats afraid to be labeled "soft on drugs"—and so a marijuana grower can land in prison for life without parole while a murderer might be in for eight years: no rational person can defend this; it is a Dostoyevskian nightmare and it exists only because politicians fled in the face of danger. That includes Bill Clinton, under whose administration the prosecution of Americans for marijuana went up hugely so that now there are more folks in prison for marijuana than for violent crimes. More than for manslaughter or rape. This only makes sense in the fantasy world of Washington, where perception counts for more than reality. To an old Democrat, who takes a ground view of politics—What is the actual effect of this action on the lives of real people?—it is a foul tragedy that makes you feel guilty about enjoying your freedom. Here I am, drinking coffee in a café in St. Paul and tolerating this shameful savagery in our midst. If the state cuts off your right hand with a meat cleaver on my account and I don't object, then it is my cleaver and my fingerprints on it. I don't dare visit Sandstone Federal Prison for fear of what I'd find there. People who chose marijuana, a more benign drug than alcohol, and got caught in the religious war that we Democrats in a weak moment signed on to. God help us if we form alliances with such bullies as would destroy a kid's life for raising cannabis plants.

Nonetheless, for all I can say against Democrats, we are the party that upholds the generous spirit even when we ourselves are mean. We are the party that respects the individual, believing that each American is complicated, poetic, full of mystery and genius, capable of profound love, also capable of meanness, which makes it important for politics to be charitable lest we unleash the mob. This is never far away, the crowds with torches howling for the Jews or blacks or Mormons or Japanese.

I became a Democrat because I was eager and hopeful, not because I was angry. Anger makes for fine radio but the shelf life is short. It's a crummy way to live. Your mother was right: forgive and forget. Live in the present and you'll be happier. Your old bachelor uncle Art who camps in his easy chair grumbling about the New Deal and how the Depression was a hoax and anybody who wanted to work could get a job but no, the Gummint came in with its WPA (We Poke Along) to reward the indolent, and Pearl Harbor was arranged by that drunken womanizer Roosevelt to get us into the war, and we shouldn't have been fighting Hitler anyway, Stalin was the real enemy, which you wouldn't know from reading the papers because they're all owned by Jews—you wouldn't want this dear man to be put in charge of anything that matters. Let him wave a flag at the Fourth of July parade, but don't let him give a speech and embarrass your kids. And don't put him in charge of the lunch: leave that to people who can run things. In Minnesota we had an angry skinhead governor named Jesse "the Body" Ventura who slouched into office on 37% of the vote and turned out to be an opportunist whose first act in office was to sell the book rights. He was a troubled soul, thin-skinned, a growler and ranter and snit thrower. After four years of him it was a relief to go back to politics as usual, where soft-spoken people with ordinary chest sizes sit down and negotiate and get the job done. He was a professional wrestler, used to working within a simple story structure, but politics isn't a story, it's a process. It's not about confrontation and threat and revenge and triumph. It's mostly about civility. Most men and women in politics are there because they genuinely care about people and want to do good things in their behalf. Most people who ever saw it up close came away impressed.

WHAT DO-GOODER DEMOCRATS HAVE DONE FOR YOU

*

Civil Rights. In 1960, when I entered college, colored folk sat in the rear and white folk in the front in cities all across the South. The drinking fountains, the schools, the churches, the polling places, American apartheid evident everywhere. People marched in the streets to claim the right to vote and faced state troopers who stormed them with clubs and tear gas. And when the marchers sang "We Shall Overcome," simple decency told you to sing with them. In the North, white people and black people tended to be careful how they mingled and what they said to each other. Some friends and I played basketball against a black team at Phyllis Wheatley settlement house in north Minneapolis and it was terrifying to me, even though no hostile words were said or gestures made. I was scared simply because they were black. One black boy attended our school, Lincoln Berry, with whom we had a distant, painfully polite acquaintance. Integration changed American life and made it possible to mingle less self-consciously.

Jimmy Carter was prospering in Plains, Georgia, and owned a fertilizer plant and a peanut shellery and warehouses, and then the White Citizens Council pressured him to join their crusade and boycotted him when he refused, which stuck in his craw and got him interested in running for governor. He didn't like to be pushed around by arrogant guys who poke a finger in your sternum and tell you what to think. Like the colonial ancestors who got pushed and poked by the royal governors and then started to poke back. He stands in stark contrast to Strom Thurmond, the segregationist and father of a child by a young black servant of his family, who felt quite at home in the Republican Party. You didn't need to preach segregation in the Republican Party—it was already in force and it still is. In the Sixties, Republicans seized a great political opportunity and locked Abraham Lincoln in the closet and took up Stephen Douglas's flag of states' rights ("I care more for the great principle of self-government . . . and the great inalienable rights of white men . . . than I do for all the Negroes in Christendom"), which carried the Republicans to power in one national election after another. What exactly it is that Republicans have done for the South other than wave the flag and quote Scripture, I don't know. What Democrats did was accelerate change. You can talk about problems of race until you're blue in the face, but it's simply true that for most white Americans, color is no longer a big factor in everyday life. An African American who grew up in the Midwest among Christian people—he and I have more in common than I have with my white liberal Unitarian friend from Cambridge. Much more. I envy my Unitarian friend his cool but the gospel-breathing black guy from St. Paul is much more my brother. God looks on the heart, as he and I know, and the power of guilt is greater than the fact of race.

Girls with Ponytails. A girl today can look forward to a life of such opportunity as her old grandmother hardly dared imagine back in 1960. Betty Friedan did her part along with other big brassy women, the 1963 Presidential Commission on the Status of Women recognized the fact of sex discrimination, and in 1972

Congress passed Title IX legislation making it illegal to discriminate against women in employment and in education, including sports, and from this came the legions of lean girls with ponytails tearing around the basketball courts and soccer fields of America. The self-confidence and discipline and physical joy of sports were not so available to the girls I went to high school with. Girls who loved games beyond puberty were thought to be odd, mannish, unattractive. Today, you see dads in the bleachers who jump up and cheer their daughters with great feeling, Republican or Democrat—American dads have become feminists in behalf of their daughters, a tidal change for which you should thank the Democratic Party, like it or not. Girls who aren't feminists have risen on the same tide as girls who are, the Southern Baptist Confederate Republican girls of Greenville and Waco have risen along with the leftist granola girls of Cambridge and Berkeley. The women who agitated for sexual equality and the men who listened to them first were Democrats. Republicans would have been content to have the ladies make lunch and be winsome and deferential. Thanks to Democrats, your daughter can think about going to medical school or pushing off into the corporate shark tank or choice C or D or E, and the world seems more normal with women circulating freely in it. Young women today don't tiptoe around men or avert their eyes like vestal virgins; they speak up and expect to be heard. Men and women mingle more or less unselfconsciously as equals and a man who cannot deal with this is considered weird.

Clean Air. No-smoking laws: a major intrusion by do-gooders into people's lives, and pity the poor office workers huddled in doorways smoking, but almost everyone sees it as a step forward, away from the smoky classrooms and offices of my youth, and a kindness to us all. I smoked Luckies and Pall Malls, three packs a day for twenty years, and quit before the posse arrived, a good thing because I would have hated being sent outdoors to smoke, but in the end, I would have gone, grousing and complaining, and eventually quit. They say you can't legislate behavior, and maybe you can't, but you sure can give it a push in the right direction. Or so Democrats believe.

Geezerhood. If we're lucky, we get old, and there is more dignity in old age today, thanks to Medicare. Ask my mother: she's 91 and lives in her old home among her mementos, putting one foot ahead of the other, stubbornly independent, whereas her father languished in a nursing home in his old age and saw his savings dribble away and died at 73. She has arthritis and various other ailments, and life is diminished on account of them—she doesn't drive a car or garden (except for the plants on her deck) or whomp up big dinners and she takes great care navigating a snowy sidewalk—but life is pretty good. She sits in her old living room and looks out at the lawn that was a cornfield when Dad dug the basement in 1947 and built the house board by board and planted spindly trees that grew into a grove of giants, where her six little kids tore around and where a solid double off the bat of cousin Don smashed the picture window in the summer of 1954. Fifty Christmas trees have stood in that corner of the living room. Dozens of children in graduation gowns were photographed in that room. Grandbabies were brought there to be adored. Dad died in the downstairs bedroom. And one large cornerstone in her life is Medicare, which, for the grand sum of $58.70 a month, gives her quick access to physicians, a visit to the emergency room if need be, even a trip to the Mayo Clinic to see why she is feeling so fatigued these days. She ran up about $5,000 in medical bills last year, of which she paid only $146.

I would gladly pay her bills but then she'd need to involve me in her decisions and would lose some of her privacy, a precious thing to my mother, who fought off colon cancer and chose not to say much about it. If I were her benefactor, she would feel she was a burden.

Medicare is the creation of Democrats and it has changed old age. If you're old, you aren't expected to accept pain and misery as your cross to bear and sit quietly by the window and sink uncomplaining into the dark. You're allowed to totter off to a clinic and claim the attention of a doctor and recite your complaints and hope to feel better. "I have trouble breathing. My knees hurt." Well, let's have a look. If you're 90 and really hoping for five more good years, we'll do what we can for you. Maybe you can have ten. If you're depressed, ask your doctor about drugs, and if you need help to function sexually, ask about that. Even if you're 80.

This is new. Medicare says that even though you're not working and may need special help with the ordinary business of life, nonetheless you have value in this society. This is a Democratic idea. Be a howling right-winger if it gives you pleasure, but nonetheless milk comes from cows and Medicare comes from Democrats.

Pregnant Teens. Legal abortion is due to *Roe v. Wade*, not to Democrats, but we have defended it, even those of us with moral reservations about it. As the teen pregnancy rate declines and the abortion rate along with it, we can see the day approaching when this angry issue recedes, and we pro-choice Democrats can reconcile with our natural allies in the Catholic Church. The Church is morally offended by abortion and it is also offended by poverty and social injustice in ways that Republicans never could be: to oppose abortion, as they do, and also promote low wages and harass welfare mothers and hack away at public services—this is moral dishonesty that staggers the mind. This is stepping on the drowning woman's hand as she grabs on to the gunwale.

As long as we have pregnant girls of 12 and 13 and 14, there will be abortion. For them, and for others, the prospect of parenthood is grim beyond words. A 13-year-old girl is too young to be a mother, and if she is living in poverty with an angry drug-addled mother of her own, she doesn't stand much chance of bringing up a healthy child and having any decent life herself. So, rather than leave her to suffer the consequences of her behavior, we allow the drastic and merciful step of abortion of the embryo. The pro-lifers who demonstrate at Planned Parenthood clinics and hold up pictures of bloody fetuses should rather hold up signs with the number of hours per week they're volunteering for child care.

We live in a culture that so exploits sexuality that little kids grow up in a red-light district, even suburban and small-town kids. Kids get wired early on into sexual roles, girls of 9 and 10 dress like streetwalkers, and it isn't left-wing academics who are selling this to them, it is corporate America, and it's the symbiotic link between puritans and pornographers (similar to that between prohibitionists and bootleggers) that makes the game go round. Janet Jackson's right tit, exposed on national TV at the Super Bowl, was the talk of the nation, more in bemusement—after all, the woman had products to promote—but the usual voices of shock and dismay were raised, thus raising the promotional value. Why do Republicans not get this? Their sulfurous views about sex, their obsession over it, make the game more titillating, and so, in the United States, girls under 15 are at least five times more likely to get pregnant than girls the same age in secular Europe where sex is viewed as an ordinary part of life and nothing to huff and puff about. A little secularism might help. If your daughter were 15 and pregnant, scared to death, weeping, angry at herself, embarrassed, you would do what you had to do to do right by her. You would not send her to the Reverend Falwell. You would not throw her to the winds to drift into depression and despair and deliver her child in a toilet and leave it in a Dumpster to die. And you wouldn't want anybody else's daughter to drift that way either.

Oddballs. Mental illness is not the shameful secret it used to be—if you suffer from depression, if you're a recovering alcoholic, if your kid is autistic, you can look other people in the eye and say so and expect them to be decent about it. You just say, "I'm bipolar," or "My son is schizophrenic," or "My daughter has apraxia," and that is that. "Oh," they say, and you talk about it, or you don't, and life goes on. We don't lock them in attics anymore, thanks to generations of progressive reformers such as Dorothea Dix, a recovering Calvinist. She was brought up thinking that mental illness was God's punishment for unspeakable sin—then she saw crazy people chained in dank penitentiaries and she changed her mind and devoted her life to campaigning for compassion and mercy. This can't be chalked up to Democrats, though Democrats nowadays are more likely to fund the programs. Yes, perhaps the country has swung too far toward confessionalism, maybe we have too many syndromes, but mental illness needs to be named and acknowledged so it can be accepted and put in its proper place and life can go on. I often think of Lonnie and Ronnie and Dorby, my old classmates who were different, slower, more lumpish—we didn't know what was wrong, nobody said; we weren't supposed to ask— and then, somewhere in junior high school, they simply vanished. Where did they go? What was their problem? Nobody would say. It's different now.

Cops. Law enforcement is better. Way better. Cops are more likely to be trained, disciplined professionals and not schoolyard bullies in a uniform. They look more like us and less like a Moose lodge. Those old bull elephants are gone. The Iowa state patrolman who pulled me over late one night years ago told me to get out and lie facedown on the shoulder of the road while he radioed my license plate number to headquarters, and twenty minutes later told me to get up and get the hell out. My offense—I knew it and he knew that I knew it—was that I had long hair. That sort of cop is gone. In St. Paul, if your car has been broken into, you get prompt service: the officer comes to your door, fills out the forms, gives you some tips on prevention, and gives you a cop's view of what's going on in the neighborhood these days. You feel well served. The result is greater respect for the law, which is just common sense: that's our badge on their chests, our lives and property that hang in the balance. Republicans have a dark urge to privatize the police, which is yet one more of their disastrous ideas: law enforcement is not a business, it is a calling, a pure public service. Sensible Democrats know this.

Tolerance. Make fun of PC to your heart's content, but there is less outright cruelty toward the vulnerable in everyday life. Some jokes aren't funny anymore. We are doubly protective of children. The sadistic Mr. Lewis who beat some of the boys in my school would not operate with such a free hand today. The big boss doesn't lean up against the young receptionist the way he might have in years past. All the ramps that got carved into curbs at intersections, according to federal specs in the Americans with Disabilities Act of 1990, for people in wheelchairs (also a boon to parents pushing strollers and kids on bikes): that's new, a little monument to sensitivity. The ADA, like the gay rights movement, was built on the women's movement, which was built on the civil rights movement, which gave us the Civil Rights Act of 1964, a large moment in American history. In my youth, you heard respectable men tell jokes about Hebes and Yids and coons and niggers, and then came the Montgomery bus boycott and Greensboro and the first sit-in, February 1, 1960, and things changed. Not everything, but many things. Decent people don't wink at racism anymore. The country is more tolerant. Gay men and women are neighbors, friends, relatives. Two women arrive at the party together, introduce themselves as partners: people are okay with this. No need to discuss it. We remember the old bachelor uncles, the furtive nocturnal disappearances, the weeping and recriminations, the secret family meetings—no need for all that—if you're gay, be gay. A window is opened and a fresh breeze blows in.

*

There is prejudice still, but not so implacable, it can be worked around, teased, poked, prodded. Most Americans feel there is something screwy about a person who can't relate to his fellow humans of any color. This is in the American tradition of tolerance going back to 1654, when the Dutch of New Amsterdam forbade public worship except in the Dutch Reformed Church, but when a shipload of Jews arrived from Brazil and held the first Rosh Hashanah service, the authorities said: *Well, all right. Go ahead. It's no skin off my nose. Whatever. It's a big country. Who am I to judge?* That's the American spirit. Republicans don't seem to understand that.

*

These long civilizing strides were aided and abetted by government—government big enough to have impact, with a capable bureaucracy to work patiently through cumbersome due process and accomplish incremental change—all done, not out of anger but for the love of liberty. Tidal changes in the North and South, among Republicans and Democrats alike. Most Americans pay very little attention to public policy—we gave it up in favor of music and games and barbecue and necking in dark places, the pursuit of happiness—but nonetheless we are part of a social compact and expect our representatives to defend it. If they chop holes in the compact, there will come a day of reckoning.

The gaping hole in the compact is health care—42 million Americans have no health insurance and must jump through hoops in order to get treatment. I know, I used to be one of them, when I was writing fiction for the *New Yorker* and scraping along and had to take my wife twice to General Hospital in Minneapolis for treatment. Exquisite humiliation. Go to any inner-city emergency room and see suffering people filling out forms about their finances and waiting hour after hour after hour, a primitive caste system of medicine in a Christian country. National health insurance would simplify the system. The sick will be treated eventually—they won't be left to die in the streets—so why not do it in a humane fashion with a modicum of dignity? We've left the dark fatalistic age of medicine when the doc was a kindly old coot who held your hand as you expired. Penicillin came in and other antibiotics to fight infection and surgery took great leaps forward and now if interesting problems show up on the CAT scan we do not faint and fall over, we set out to fight the disease—and in this nation where tax-supported research propelled these great advances, our denial of the benefits to so many is downright stone-hearted. There is health care for Republican dogs and cats superior to what people get in the charity ward. Health care is a fundamental right: you go flying heedless through your youth on waxen wings, immune to illness, immortal, but then you fall to earth and need to be cared for and not lie broken on the gurney waiting for the accountants upstairs to decide if you're entitled to attention.

Mortality is the ultimate democracy. The tramp and the Trump are susceptible to the same bad news at the doctor's office: each man's prostate is as vulnerable as any other's. You go to the Mayo Clinic in Rochester and sit in a beige waiting room among women in Armani suits, dairy farmers, assorted geezers and geezerettes of Olmsted County, pooh-bahs and nabobs chatting on cell phones, here and there an oil sheikh, and all of us praying the same continuous silent prayer: *O Great Internist, let the tests come out clean and please no colonoscopy today and no referral to a urologist.* You imagine some pea-sized tumor in your innards that has sprouted and sent its tendrils shooting through the lymph nodes and now dense jungle growths have a grip on your vitals and in a few months people will sit in an Episcopal church and softly weep for you and plant your ashes in the ground and go have a nice lunch. We all brood over this. We are all equal in our dread of the end to this delightful life and our disbelief in our own mortality. It will be a great day in America when we finally see that everybody can come see the doctor as needed, not be shunted to the back door and the charity ward.

Chapter 8

❋ ○ ○ ○ ○ ○ ○ ○ ○ ۞ ○ ○ ○ ○ ○ ○ ○ ○ ❋

AT THE CAFÉ

A liberal lady of DC
By day was tasteful and PC,
And then after ten
She went out with men
Who were rednecks, vulgar and greasy.
"When it comes to the masculine specie,"
She said, "Believe me, I'm easy,
But liberal guys
Tend to theologize
And I am not St. Clare of Assisi."

WHEN I AM gloomy about politics, I go sit alone in a crowded café in my neighborhood in St. Paul where art students like to hang out, intense young people with uncertain prospects in life, and old gaffers and

135

loafers and tourists from the suburbs, genteel bohemi-
ans dreaming of the Dead and how it was to be 20 and
discover Prévert and Camus. And some allrightniks like
me. I sit and inhale the smell of coffee amid the murmur
of Midwestern voices like water lapping on the shore. A
true comfort on a cold day in April. I feel attached to
this neighborhood, having lived here off and on half my
life. Today, the morning paper makes me feel I'm living
in the Austro-Hungarian Empire of 1914 with Arch-
duke George in his plumed helmet strolling the palace
grounds, but a walk around the neighborhood can cure
the blues. The trees are budding, lilac bushes too, girls
with bare midriffs stroll past. An ugly nursing home
has been demolished, new condos coming in. Summit
Hill was Millionaires Row, home of the upper crust, an
old Republican bailiwick of lumber and insurance and
railroad families of the Gilded Age, houses that, after a
century of graceful decline, were bought up and reno-
vated by Democrats. Liberals have a secret lust for Vic-
toriana. I've been in plenty of these old manses with
their screen porches and bay windows and turrets and
piazzas and arches, attending fund-raisers for losing
liberals. And some winners, including Bruce Vento, a

modest hardworking guy with enormous eyebrows who represented St. Paul in Congress for 24 years and did good things for the homeless and for the American wilderness, fought the good fights and then came home to die of lung cancer. And Senator Paul Wellstone, who once lived around here with his wife, Sheila. A September afternoon and fifty people standing around on a brick backyard terrace at fifty bucks a head (discounts available), a dozen bottles of $10 Chardonnay and a tub of Leinenkugels on ice, baskets of chips, chip dip, salsa, and an earnest DFL candidate standing on the back steps, jabbing the air and talking passionately about workers' compensation, and I look around and see my people, people who were milling around the St. Paul Auditorium that night in 1984 when Walter Mondale, flushed like a middleweight after a fifteen-rounder, came out to concede to Ronald Reagan. We all remember the miserable defeat of George McGovern, and the Dukakis debacle, the fall of Gore in the swamp of Florida, the fall of Kerry—one godawful moment after another. At present, we are in our usual disarray and widely ridiculed by angry menopausal males who equate dissent with treason, but we Democrats do not faint at the sound of hecklers. The only shame is to lose heart. So we gather in the backyard, put our money in the plastic bucket, and give each other heart. I notice the tall guy with black hair falling over his eyes. It's Barry Halper, my patron saint from University days, now a big man in satellite radio, and we commiserate about getting old and rant about the dang Republicans, and pat each other's shoulders, and two years later we'll meet in another backyard and hear another candidate jab the air and talk about health insurance, using three or four acronyms per sentence, which is Greek to me, but I'm a Democrat, confusion and ignorance do not discourage me.

This café is owned by locals, which we old bleedingheart Democrats prefer to patronize, being romantic about small entrepreneurs. We would walk past a Starbucks to see if maybe there was a Stella's or a Stanley's on the next block. The little guy who mortgages his house to open a business—that hits us where we live. My cousin used to sell vegetables out of a pickup truck at the farmers' market and he grew his truck garden into a big greenhouse operation north of here, a kind and honest man, the hero of the family. Another cousin launched a software company and a third is a one-man architectural firm, designing fine churches and libraries, and another is a tire dealer, and I am a writer and the founder of *A Prairie Home Companion*, which is produced by a small independent company. Not unusual for the descendants of farmers to opt for independence.

The coffee shop is a big L-shaped room with exposed brick walls and arches, a woman-sized copy of the Statue of Liberty. The front window is steamed up; an April cold front has moved in. The coffee menu is on the wall above the cash register: espresso, latte, cappuccino, mocha, Americano in three sizes and all sorts of permutations, 2% or skim or whole, a variety of syrups, chocolate dust, cinnamon. Biscotti, croissants, bagels, and four kinds of muffins in a glass case. Behind the case, a girl in a white apron studies me, a tall attitudinous girl. Her cropped dark hair is tinged with neon blue, silver rings dangle in her eyebrows, a stud glitters in her nose, and she gives me a look of offended nobility and waits for my order. She is an artist, surely. Who else would need to be so prickly? God gives to the vulnerable a great power of disdain to ward off predators. I smile at her—I'm on your side, Babes—but she doesn't buy it. She grimaces. Come on, Pops, pick your muffin. I choose bran and a tall Americano.

A good hangout. You come in, you feel you could spend the day. The music today tends toward old blues, bottleneck guitar. Ethel Waters, Bessie Smith, Arthur Crudup. Artistly people and some writerlies and some law students slumming. Some older laptop people camp here who work at home as I do and maybe miss the office camaraderie. A gaunt beauty with chestnut hair taps away on her laptop, glancing up at the door. White jeans, purple striped stockings, yellow jersey, sunglasses parked on her head. (Not from here. LA maybe, or Minneapolis.) The laptop is the best thing for writers since the opposable thumb, a portable typewriter that doubles as a file cabinet and a spelling editor and a reference room. Students sit in twos and threes, slumped, leaning on each other, talking through their noses, and two UPS drivers on their lunch hour, and a man teaching his little towheaded boy to play chess. Two old guys are engaged in cribbage, who I guess might be between jobs right now, and coming to grips with the fact that the new job will be a step down. One is a scrawny old dude,

balding, bespectacled, beige sweater and tweed jacket
and jeans, rubber shoes, maybe an old English teacher
about to embark on a new career as a cashier in a
parking ramp. A boy in a red T-shirt engrossed in the
Norton Anthology of English Literature and his raven-
haired girlfriend next to him, a darling such as Yeats
would have been crazy about for twenty years. *I will
arise, and go now, and attend the coffee shop, And sit
next to that astonishment with black hair, And the bees
and the voices of Democrats like water lapping, And the
purple glow of her beauty there.* She has a laptop too
and I wish I could read over her shoulder and find out
what someone so beautiful sounds like when she is serious. Her long dark lashes and her French mouth, her
swan neck, her hair. If I were her college professor, I'd
have to teach with my glasses off. She and Mr. Norton
clearly are a pair and I believe this is not a good day for
their romance. He goes for a refill and doesn't bother to
ask if she'd like anything. When he returns, he doesn't
touch her shoulder and her smile up at him is tentative.
On the way home, she will turn to him and say, "I'm
thinking maybe I'll go down to Chicago for a few days
and visit Hillary." And he'll say, "Fine." And she'll come

back from Chicago with a clearer view of things, re-
solved to move out of the apartment. When you've broken up a few times yourself, you can recognize the signs
of breakage in others. It's interesting watching people in
a café. Everybody has a story and some you'd give anything to be able to hear. Couples in love and couples
falling out of love and it tugs at you as nothing on TV
ever could. The old English teacher going to work at the
parking ramp: this could have happened to me, I think,
and a small voice says: *It still could, Buster.*

One thing I like about this café is the feeling, walking
in here, that everyone else in the room has babysat for
money, hitchhiked, had a few head-on encounters with
liquor, and done hard physical labor. The summer I was
15, I picked potatoes for a month, bending down all day,
filling one gunnysack after another, until I couldn't
stand up straight. It's useful to remember that when
you're older and sitting at a desk, and also how, after a
day in the potato fields, you'd play touch football until
dusk and fall into bed and be back to work at 8 A.M.
ready to go. Hard labor is an experience you have in
common with the others. No particular virtue in it, but
it's a checkpoint we all passed. The American Brother-

hood of Potato Workers lying on the cool grass under the tree at 5 P.M., straightening their backs, rinsing the dust out of their mouths with a bottle of Grain Belt. I wouldn't have missed it. We all were in the same boat, all brought up to make something of ourselves and Don't Be a Noise with Legs. Do Your Part. Don't Be a Crybaby. Pull Your Weight. Be a Good Worker. In Minnesota, we know what that means: It means to stick with the job though you're beat and your back aches. You rest and then you get up and go back to work. You don't let the others carry your load. This simple ethic, learned young, will help save you from becoming an empty suit. You might have some interesting peccadilloes, you might be on shaky ground theologically, but if you can keep filling the sacks with potatoes, keep moving, take your lunch break when it's time and then come back for more, and do this until harvest is done, then people will make allowances for you.

The old guys at the cribbage board grew up when I did, in the time before there was security. We didn't always lock our doors, and we often left the keys in the ignition. We thought nothing of lying down in a public park and taking a snooze. There were not hermetic safety seals on things. Back then people might poison a loved one but nobody would poison a perfect stranger. Now even shampoo comes with a little silver foil seal. We knew nothing of hair poisoning back in the day. And when you walked into the drugstore, there wasn't the miserable man in the fake police uniform and the headset standing at the door and glowering at the customers.

Back then we all thought of America as one nation where everybody ate turkey with sage stuffing for Thanksgiving and after dinner the kids went outside and played Starlight Moonlight and tore around till they were out of breath and came in and watched the *Bell Telephone Hour* on TV with Robert Merrill and Patrice Munsel singing Rodgers and Hammerstein and dancers making geometric shapes on the floor and then a hot rod honked and your cousin Betty came downstairs and stood in the hall and primped and spritzed some Evening in Paris behind her ears and the boy in the two-toned Chevy with the fender skirts honked again and you heard his radio playing and it wasn't the Bell Telephone Orchestra but something with a lot more drums and bass and his cigarette glowed and his hair was sculpted high on his head. He was trying out the Jimmy Dean look, but you knew his family so you didn't worry. He wasn't really bad, just young, full of piss and vinegar. You watched the show and went up to bed and left the door unlocked for Betty.

We are stoics in this room and can tolerate considerable misery without comment. Winter is long and Scandinavians can be sour and stubborn and Minnesota drivers are dangerous and you can't buy wine in a grocery store and the bars close early and the downtowns languish and the suburbs sprawl for fifty miles in all directions and commuting is brutal, and politicians are shortsighted and mosquitoes are enormous and yet, if that's what it takes to keep out the Texans, then we're happy.

If I were cheating on my taxes or dumping green gunk in the Mississippi or willfully exposing my employees to mortal danger or drawing enormous subsidies from the public trough, I wouldn't feel at ease in this café—I'd prefer to drink my coffee in a private club with a uniformed doorman lest some old crone walk over and spit in my eye. We café-goers on this cold spring day are united in a civil compact and we know it. This compact is powerful in the Midwest, thanks to our German and Scandinavian forebears, people of the *bund*, people who looked out for each other. And when we Midwesterners travel to New York or London or Paris, we wonder: if we were struck by a car and lay bleeding in the gutter, would people stop and help? The answer, surely, is yes, but here in the Midwest, there would be no question.

One morning three years ago, I heard a shriek from upstairs, a long high-pitched primeval wail, and there was my wife on the landing, holding the stiff body of our little girl. I dashed up and took Maia in my arms and Jenny went to call 911. The child was unconscious, her breathing shallow. She went into convulsions in my arms and her body stiffened, her mouth clamped shut. I thought she was dying. Sheer silent terror on a pleasant spring morning: my four-year-old daughter dying. And in about two minutes the St. Paul fire department paramedics arrived at the door. They came in, four of them, and lifted her out of my arms. They laid her on the floor and tended to her, took her temperature (she was running a fever), put an oxygen mask on her face. One of them began explaining to me about febrile convulsions, how common they are in small children, which Jenny knew about but I didn't, and then I noticed that I was still in my underwear. I pulled on a pair of trousers and we rode off to the hospital and in short order she was okay again.

The rescue squad can get to you anywhere in St. Paul in four minutes or less. That is official policy. These folks came racing up the hill from downtown, about a mile away, but there are EMTs or paramedics at eleven of the sixteen fire stations in the city and they do about eighty runs a day. The EMTs have taken a basic course of 250 class hours, the paramedics a two-year course of more than 1,000, and they know what they're doing. They work alternate 12-hour days for a week—then take four days off, then alternate 12-hour days for another week, then six days off—for an average workweek of 56 hours. They start at $38,000 a year and after three years become journeymen and jump to $50,000. The shift starts at 8 A.M., but most of them come half an hour early to sit around and drink coffee and get ready. When you call and the dispatcher sends the alarm, the paramedics are in the truck and out the door in thirty seconds. The 911 system went into service in the Twin Cities in December 1982, paid for out of the state's general fund. But the paramedics and EMTs are St. Paul city employees. And the four-minute-or-less response represents the nature of our civil compact here in St. Paul: if you urgently need help, someone will be there before panic sets in. In the suburbs, thanks to Republicans and their code of personal responsibility, the coronary victim will have time to read the entire Gospel of St. Mark before help arrives. There is a message here: if lower taxes are your priority over human life, then we know what sort of person you are. The response to a cry for help says a lot about us as human beings. You're at a party late one night and there's a scream from out on the street, and some people stick their heads out to see if there's trouble and other people don't bother. Maybe they'd rather not know.

A few years ago, a couple who lived across the hall from us in New York came to Sunday dinner at our apartment and during dinner the husband felt dizzy and excused himself and went back across the hall where he had a stroke. His wife found him, dazed, unable to speak, a few minutes later and called me and I went over to sit with him as we waited for the ambulance. It was a long wait. Malcolm was a handsome old Scot who was quite dashing in kilts at the annual Robert Burns Night and loved their vacations on the Isle of Harris, and in his last long minutes of awareness, he lay across his bed with great dignity and looked at the door, waiting for the angel. Eventually, the paramedics arrived and bundled him over to the East Side to the hospital. By the time we arrived, forty minutes had passed. Perhaps a swifter response wouldn't have made much difference. I don't know. He died a few days later.

A Democrat knows that the leaf turns and in the human comedy we are one day spectators and the next day we're in the clown act. The gains in life come slowly and the losses come on suddenly. You work for years to get your life the way you want it and buy the big house and the time-share on Antigua and one afternoon you're run down by a garbage truck and lie in the intersection, dazed, bloodied, your leg unnaturally bent, and suddenly life becomes challenging for six months. In the *Prairie Home* office, one summer evening a woman walked out the door to go home and was swarmed by wasps and staggered back into the building, bitten so badly that her air passage was swollen half shut. She was almost unconscious, going into shock, and collapsed in the hallway. Luckily, a colleague had stayed late at work and she called 911, and in came the St. Paul paramedics to save Deb's life. Every day at work, I see a bright young woman whose memorial service I might have attended had circumstances been ever so slightly different.

Two blocks from the office lived a brilliant young professor of Middle East Studies who had given birth to a little girl with Down syndrome who could not nurse and needed to be fed through a tube stuck down her nasal passage. One morning, the mother, depressed though taking antidepressants, feeling hopeless, brokenhearted at the child's misery, exhausted to the point of derangement, cut the infant's throat with a butcher knife. The mother was arrested and put in Ramsey County Jail where, a few weeks later, she managed to get a plastic garbage bag, place it over her head, tie it tight around her neck, and suffocate herself. This happened in St. Paul, Minnesota, two blocks from the office where I sit and write silly songs and Guy Noir sketches. In St. Paul, people could not get this tragedy off their minds for a long time. Long after we stopped talking about it—What more could be said?—it haunted our consciences, these two souls who had slipped through our fingers and plunged to their deaths. Somehow we could have saved them. What else, dear Lord, should we have done?

The fear of catastrophe could chill the soul but the social compact assures you that if the wasps come after you, if gruesome disease strikes down your child, if you find yourself hopelessly lost, incapable, drowning in despair, running through the rye toward the cliff, then the rest of us will catch you and tend to you and not only your friends but We the People in the form of public servants. This is a basic necessity in a developed society. Men and women make love and have babies in the knowledge that if the baby should be born with cerebral palsy or Down syndrome or a hole in its heart and require heroic care, the people of Minnesota and of St. Paul will stand with you in your dark hour. If you are saddled with trouble too great for a person to bear, you will not be left to perish by the roadside in darkness. Without that assurance, we may as well go live in the woods and take our chances.

This is Democratic bedrock: we don't let people lie in the ditch and drive past and pretend not to see them dying. Here on the frozen tundra of Minnesota, if your neighbor's car won't start, you put on your parka and get the jumper cables out and deliver the Sacred Spark that starts their car. Everybody knows this. The logical extension of this spirit is social welfare and the myriad government programs with long dry names all very uninteresting to you until you suddenly need one and then you turn into a Democrat. A liberal is a conservative who's been through treatment.

To the hard-assed redneck Republican tax cutter of the suburbs, human misery is all a fiction, something out of novels, stories of matchstick people. He's doing fine so what's the problem? He is oblivious. George Custer knew more about the Sioux than this guy knows about the world around him. He is heavily into postponement for short-term savings and long-term disaster. He and his fellow Republicans slash the funding of social welfare programs—which has instant political appeal: ENCOURAGE RESPONSIBILITY, CUT WELFARE, SAVE $$$$$—and lo and behold, children in abusive homes can no longer be removed from those homes by social workers because there's no money to pay for alternative care, and one morning, the rednecks read in the paper about a child locked in a closet for weeks, half starved, lying in its own feces, and they don't make the connection between their politics and the evil done to that child. The child's suffering has nothing to do with them. So the kid goes to relatives who also have a history of abuse. It's no skin off the redneck's nose. He's got a giant TV, 99 channels of cable, a snowmobile, a Hummer, a collection of guns, a boat, Jet Skis—he's sitting pretty. The demise of somebody else's kid at the hands of a drunken uncle is nothing but roadkill to him. This is the screw-you philosophy that festers under cover of modern Republicanism.

Part of the civil compact is the government that we install in office: if you and I subscribe to the compact, then I cannot tolerate a government that brutalizes you on my behalf. If suddenly on a Friday night the red lights flash and the cops yank your teenage son and his little envelope of marijuana into the legal meat grinder and some bullet-headed prosecutor decides to flex his muscle and charge your teenager, because he had a .22 rifle in his upstairs bedroom closet, with a felony involving use of a firearm, which under our brutal sentencing code means he can be put on ice for twenty years, and the prosecutor goes at him hammer and tongs and convinces a passive jury and your boy's life is sacrificed so that this creep can run for Congress next year—this is not your cross alone to bear; this violates the compact between you and me. Our war on drugs is a religious war against a pleasure-seeking minority and if your son is caught in it, like a raccoon in a bear trap, this gross injustice makes it hard for you to sit in a café with me if I turn a blind eye to what happened. If your life is blighted by rank injustice and I don't care, then you can't be happy in my company. That's why it's unpleasant to set foot in Texas. They execute human beings there with gay abandon. They railroad them through with a dime-store defense and the governor glances at the appeal and denies it and the defendant is tied to a gurney and put down like a dog. This fact leaves a sour cloud over Austin and Fort Worth and San Antonio, a grain of sand in the burrito, a lurid orange glow at the dance.

Narcissism and cruelty are twins: we expect God to cut us slack and hold others to account. And our criminal justice system easily turns sadistic: those people in handcuffs are not us. The state of Wisconsin has brought back the old chain gang and put radio-controlled stun belts on the prisoners so that a guard or trusty can flick a switch and impart a jolt of electricity that knocks a prisoner off his feet. You would not do this to anybody you knew personally, but when it comes to despised groups, we are capable of great cruelty in the name of toughness. Call a man a terrorist and you can lock him up for years without a trial, torture him, sodomize him, beat him to death if you wish. People campaign for office on their ability to be vicious to select groups of people unlikely to vote in large numbers.

There is a basic faith here in this café: if you work hard and pay attention and don't let the greasy tentacles of alcohol or drugs wrap around you and don't take stupid shortcuts that land you in jail, you can thrive, and if catastrophe falls on you, earthquake or drought or flood or fire, the others will come to your rescue. If a wrong is done to you, it will be addressed. Maybe this is sentimental liberalism from Thomas Hart Benton murals and Carl Sandburg poems and old Hollywood flicks about the little guy, but I don't think so. It's simply the social contract by which people pledge comfort and support to each other in time of need, which each of us will sooner or later come to. If this contract is torn up, you'd need to buy a .357 pistol and a junkyard dog and head for the woods and stock up on dried foods. I have drawn on this contract often. My education at the U. My child has been blessed by loving teachers whose gifts were nurtured at state expense and she was rescued by the fire department. Three years ago after I suddenly felt wheezy and woke up in the night feeling suffocated, Dr. Orczulak at Mayo opened up my thorax and sewed a leaky valve in my heart, a dramatic procedure whose perfection over the past fifty years was heavily subsidized by the taxpaying public. Dr. Walt Lillehei of the University of Minnesota was a giant in the field, operating on blue babies and hopeless little kids with bad hearts. I saw pictures of them on the front page of the *Minneapolis Star* in the Fifties, smiling wanly from their hospital beds—a major news item back then: the heart of a living person stopped and opened with a knife and the bunged-up part mended as you would cobble a shoe—and despite high casualty rates and the enormous cost of each attempt, the open-heart operation was brought (thanks to public assistance) to the point of utter ordinariness, which my operation was. Everyone and his cousin has had a bypass, or a double, or a quadruple with a one and a half gainer. No more traumatic, on the whole, than a broken leg. Thank you, America. How could I, whose life has been extended by this largesse, turn into an angry right-winger, a knee-jerk tax cutter, flogging public employees and the very idea of public service? How could a graduate of the University of Minnesota turn around after graduation and become a No New Taxes Republican and reduce his alma mater to the level of a community college? What towering ingratitude lies at the heart of the Republican Party! What a mean-spirited betrayal of the common life of this country!

Chapter 9

✻∘○○○○○○○○○⚙○○○○○○○○✻

ORDINARY DECENCY

There was a broadcaster named Rush
Whose mind turned to marshmallow mush.
One day he declared
Pi equals E squared
And also, a pair beats a flush.

THIS MORNING in the café, a man is telling about a new floodwall the city might build to keep the St. Paul downtown airport from flooding. "One mile of sheet metal twenty feet above water. Like a giant heating duct on the Mississippi." Someone else saw Meryl Streep water-skiing on the Mississippi. Last summer. She was making a movie. She wore green sunglasses and a pink swimsuit. Someone tells about his cousin, a botanist, who got back from Iran where twenty-five thousand people died in ten minutes in an earthquake. The cousin loves the Iranian people, the culture. How old is Meryl Streep? Fifty? She is one of the world's most stunningly beautiful women. You have to wonder about an airport commission that would propose wrapping a mile of sheet metal around the bank of the river. Who do they think they are, Christo? So goes the conversation over coffee. I couldn't live in a country where strangers don't talk freely to each other and tell stories and air their grievances and joke and gas about this and that, and Republicans are trying to give us that country, where taxes are cut and services are stripped and the schools go to a four-day week and the local library depends on bake sales and user fees and police and fire are outsourced to a company that provides those services and soon 40 or 60 or 100 million Americans realize they are living in the weeds on the edge of the cliff. The civility of daily life depends on a sense of well-being. (Duh.) When the airline declares bankruptcy, the flight attendants realize that their future is shaky, their pensions might shrink in the wash, and they're not so jokey or sweet as in the old days. The corporation turns into the plantation. The field hands line up for work and Mr. George offers them

18 cents per hour and a cold potato for lunch and they accept his offer. He is the boss and under him are the managers, and then there are the field hands, who live in treehouses or the backseats of cars. The bosses have their country club, and the managers have the Elks and Kiwanis and Rotary, and the field hands are allowed to sit in the public park so long as they don't spit or use bad language or play cards or speak to women. Sometimes the boss stops by and says, "Morning, Chester," and the hand looks down at the ground and says, "Morning, Mass' George" in a low tone of voice. There is an oppressive set of reticences that apply, depending on your social calculus. You stay on your side of the line. That's not America as I know it. A house divided against itself cannot stand; we cannot long endure, half predator, half prey.

If you forgot your billfold on a table of this café in St. Paul, you could come back an hour later and the girl at the counter would hand it to you, all the cash still in it. If you need a light, a smoke, directions, a quarter for the pay phone, the use of a pen, a restaurant recommendation, travel tips, the name of a movie you're trying to think of, you can get those here, no problem. That's because we're middle-class Midwesterners. We know each other by voice. If you strip us of health insurance, this will change. On the streets of New York right after 9/11 people talked to you or talked in your vicinity and you leaned over and listened—and you heard about the cousin who stayed home from work that day, and the man with the office on the 93rd floor of the north tower who lingered over his coffee in a diner and missed being killed that day. Like most catastrophes, it was democratic—the busboys and dishwashers in Windows on the World died along with the executives—just as war used to be. On Memorial Day, the men and women of the American Legion and VFW place little flags and flowers at the graves of veterans. There isn't a Platinum Class flag for those whose families pony up more. All soldiers are unknown in the end, death is anonymous, and the old men who troop the colors are contemptuous of the neoconservative chicken hawks who never fought but enjoy speechifying about the use of American power. The old men know about the terror and confusion and stink and evil of war. The most fitting memorial observance is silence. The honor guard stands, the breeze rippling the leaves, and we think our thoughts about those boys and their real sufferings and the bugler plays Taps and we turn and go home.

All those dead boys and millions of the rest of us went through the draft board physical, once a powerful democratic checkpoint. If you were a 17-year-old boy, you thought about the approach of your 18th birthday, it had significance. If your draft board called, you went. Even a Rockefeller had to drop trousers and spread his cheeks and bend over. Of course, the great checkpoint was military service. In the U.S. Army, my dad and his buddies learned to stand in line and accept their place in the bigger picture, and they met people utterly unlike themselves and bonded with them and thereby learned something about decency.

Back in the democratic Fifties, if I needed a ride home from Anoka, I could stand on the West River Road with my thumb out and cars would come around the bend and I'd look them straight in the windshield and think positive thoughts and smile pleasantly and most cars would whoosh past but one driver would see that my clothes were clean and my posture good and he'd stop and pick me up and I got to meet interesting people that way, people unlike me, and hear some of their stories.

People might say things to a kid they'd never meet again. *Let me tell you something. Don't ever get married.* Okay. *I mean it, don't get married. It's grief from morning to night.* Yes, sir. *There is nothing you can do to make them happy. Nothing.* I see. *There is nothing you can do to please them. You go the extra mile and they're mad because you're an inch short.* And you got your ride to downtown Minneapolis. This doesn't happen much anymore. It represented the trailing edge of the Thirties spirit of mutual assistance—disaster can strike anyone at any time so we do not turn people away who need something that we can provide. Downtown, in my youth, you saw little strips of paper stuck in the cracks of brick walls or telephone poles by the streetcar stops. My mother explained that they were streetcar transfers, left by people who didn't need them for people who did. No more. In Mr. Bush's America, it's Screw You all the way. The life of freeway rush hour, among Visigoths who resent your very presence.

America has a democratic heart. It is a generous and redemptive land where you can lift your head and know that justice and equality and a decent sympathy for the underdog are part of the music and poetry of people. We

honor openness of heart, a democratic style. You are polite to the checkout lady at the Piggly Wiggly and to the
shoeshine man. You make small talk with the cabdriver.
You do not lord it over people as if you were the grand
panjandrum of Mushti and they your serfs. You don't
expect people to genuflect in your direction. The big wa-
hoo and the ribbon clerk, the barmaid and the Episcopal
bishop of Poughkeepsie—we're all in it together. It's
America, not some little comic-opera aristocracy, and if
people don't tug on their forelock when you walk into
the room, Your Eminence, don't take it too hard.

Good manners are democratic. Your mother taught
you to be kind to all whom you meet, that everyone
matters, not to look down your nose at people who aren't
dressed so beautifully as you or don't speak with your
mellifluous tones. When I run into Midwesterners in
foreign places, I notice their good manners, which aren't
about dessert forks but about kindness and the ability to
see beyond yourself. They don't bitch about the rainy
weather or the slow service or the unfamiliar food or the
language barriers, they look on the bright side.

Your mother didn't raise you to be a jerk who sucks
up to power and treats the help like dirt. Make your way

in the world, but mind your manners. And don't pick on the vulnerable. You go backstage after the Lake Wobegon High School production of *My Fair Lady* in which your niece played Eliza like a fence post all night and there she is, trembling, shaken, ashen-faced, and you say, "It was good, Lindsey. You really connected with that audience. It had so much resonance and honesty." So she doesn't torture herself over this debacle. Probably she has no talent—so what? No need to face the whole truth all at once.

Sports is a democratic world: everyone sees the ball game for himself and snaps his own mental picture of the runner sliding home, safe or out, and you give the umpire the benefit of your point of view. Up in the corporate skybox you miss the camaraderie of the bleachers and the acerbic wit of young men after a couple beers. A player earning $14 million a year—that's okay. He didn't land the job because he's the owner's nephew, he got it because he could cover his position and hit the curveball, and why shouldn't talent be rewarded? But if he bobbles an easy grounder or takes a called third strike down the middle of the plate, the bleachers will have plenty to say to him.

I sit at the ballpark and think of Gene McCarthy, the sage of Watkins, Minnesota, a man whose easy grace was misinterpreted as diffidence. He was a lanky first baseman and an Irish politician who loved to stand up in front of a crowd, stick his hands in his jacket pockets, and rock back on his heels and orate. He was succinct and funny and had a natural swing, even in old age. At the novelist J. F. Powers's funeral in Minnesota in June 1999, the priest delivered the eulogy. But the senator was not to be denied. At the funeral lunch, he leaned over and asked me if I intended to make a few remarks. I picked up the cue—"No, but I'm glad to introduce you," I said, and did, and he stood and spoke gracefully for ten minutes about Ireland and Minnesota and baseball and Jim Powers, and sat down, the old contender, in great form.

I sit in the ballpark and think of young men on the troopships sailing to North Africa and Sicily and the beaches of Normandy, fearing death and yet believing in survival. They planned to escape death and return home to live this good life, watching the ball game on a June night, eating a bratwurst slathered with mustard. Right up to the moment of death, they dreamed of this, the outfielders poised in the twilight, the little kids chasing around under the stands, the pitcher going into his stretch, checking the runner at first—a pure democracy: all batters get three strikes, the strike zone the same for everyone, also the base paths and fences.

When the old white CEO gets in a cab at the airport and looks at the young black cabdriver, sports is what they can talk about. Not their summer vacation plans, not cars, not homes, not politics. Basketball.

Then there is the democracy of jokes. Telling a joke right is a skill, like hammering a nail, and anyone can learn it. *The man walks into the bar with a handful of dog turds and says to the bartender, "Hey, look what I almost stepped in!"* Anybody can tell that joke. You join a group of strangers in a bar and listen to their jokes and wait for the opening to tell yours. *The reason men fart more than women is that women don't keep their mouths shut long enough for the pressure to build up.* You tell a simple joke simply. You deliver it dry, not too much topspin. You do the setup—*A guy takes his boy deer hunting and they're creeping through the woods*—and here you can embroider a little, and then you feed them the punch line—*and the man says, "Son, this is your first deer hunt, it's a very important time in your life, it marks your passage into manhood, do you have any questions?"* and the boy says, *"Yes. If you die of a heart attack, how do I get home?"* If you tell it well and don't oversell the joke, or apologize, or laugh more than they do, and if the joke is a new one, you'll be welcome here. *A man went to the Lutheran church on Sunday morning and after the service he stopped to shake the pastor's hand. He said, "Preacher, I'll tell you, that was a helluva sermon. Damned fine." The pastor said, "Thank you, sir, but I'd rather you didn't use that sort of language." The man said, "I was so damn impressed with that sermon I dropped a check for $10,000 in the collection plate." The pastor said, "Holy shit."*

Chapter 10

A CIVILIZED PEOPLE

There was an old liberal named Kurt
Who wore his heart on his shirt.
The poor pay of teachers
Or the death of small creatures
Left him speechless and terribly hurt.

THE BLUE-TINGED girl brings my coffee with a grand hauteur that I admire. It's that old piss-on-your-shoe spirit of the underdog class that seems so scarce these days. Corporate America is successful at training this out of people through flattery ("You are a vital member of the HellMart family") and terror ("Smile and speak in a perky voice or you'll be fired and lose your health insurance"). School tries to knock the piss and vinegar out of you, the church coaxes you to be passive and sweet, but the human spirit is resilient and the blue-tinged girl refuses to curtsy. I like those teenagers with the chopped hair and tattoos and metal stuck in their faces and dramatic clothes. It's a statement. They remind me of myself when I started to imagine I was a writer. Not much evidence of it, so what could I do but try to look the part, smoke unfiltered Luckies, practice irony, wear army surplus, and carry myself with some grandeur. Here is this girl, making maybe eight bucks an hour with tips, but with a grand attitude and a big urge to be somebody. I wish her well. I wish I could give her a word of advice: lighten up, kid.

"You want lunch?" she says. The lunch menu is written on a blackboard on the wall. Then I notice the green Wellstone pin on her shirt. "Did you know Paul?" I say. She nods. I imagine he came in here to eat and, being Paul, he reached over the counter and shook everybody's hand. I don't: I'm a writer. We hang back and observe. Paul relished life on the highways and byways, bobbing into a crowded café, encountering people. When he went out for lunch, he made a point of sticking his head in the kitchen afterward and shaking hands with the cooks and the dishwashers. I was a dishwasher once and if a U.S. Senator had appeared in the steam of the scullery and taken my hand, it would've made my day, that's for sure. You saw Paul in the Twin Cities airport, waiting to fly back to Washington, talking, a little knot of passersby around him, bouncing on the balls of his feet as he talked. He wasn't seduced by comfort and flattery and he kept his point of view as an outsider. He was a short voluble Jew who represented a state of tall laconic Scandinavians and Germans. People liked him who didn't necessarily share his opinions, because he was loyal to his people, the bus drivers, the waitresses, the dishwashers, the cleaning ladies. He wasn't a senator for rent: he spoke up for people who need speaking up for. He saw things from ground level, like a novelist, like a Democrat. He and Sheila had an apartment three blocks from here. On the morning of October 25, 2002, they drove down Selby Avenue to the downtown St. Paul airport to board the charter plane that would crash in the cold fog in the woods. That was a few years ago and the blue-tinged girl is still loyal to him. Electioneering is a combination of marathon dancing, flagpole sitting, and competitive pie eating. He'd done that for a year and he was a month away from beating his slippery opponent and getting to take a vacation with Sheila and spend time at the movies, and his pilots got off the beam and landed in the trees. He was afraid of flying and not much else. He preached against fear, as people of my generation should. We old Democrats think of them often: Paul and Sheila and daughter Marcia and their staff, Will and Mary and Tom, dying a few days before Election Day 2002.

Our beloved land has been fogged with fear—fear, the greatest political strategy ever. A drumbeat of whispered warnings and alarms to keep the public uneasy and silence the opposition. And in a time of vague fear, you can appoint bullet-brained judges, strip the bark off the Constitution, eviscerate the federal regulatory agencies, stupefy the press, lavish gorgeous tax breaks on the rich, and if anyone looks at you cross-eyed, talk about the Imminent Threat.

Meanwhile, Republicans do not much for their own people—look at the small towns of the Midwest: a fleet of sinking ships. Rural people, most of them loyal Republicans, are walking the Trail of Tears. The party's philosophy of lousy government services and corporate welfare is a disaster for the Republican voter. The number of dairy farms is in steep decline, even as milk production rises, thanks to factory farms with herds of 500 hormonally souped-up cows who put down 20,000 pounds of milk a year. Dairy farming is Republican to the core: it's very industrious people working 365 days a year. But Republican prairie towns are drying up and blowing away—the supermarket bulletin boards post notices that say ALCOHOLISM and DOMESTIC ABUSE and SUICIDE with hotlines to call for help. Meanwhile, their idea about public services and public investment is, *the less the better.* Not so different from Charles the First's. Compare this to a small town in Norway—the modern library, the swimming hall, the playing fields, the bus system—no wonder our kids are burning their brains out with crystal meth. Meanwhile, the urban bullshitters are prospering, holding their bullshit powwows in big hotel ballrooms, bloviating about Strategizing the Global Deconstruct, monkey talk, but the b.s. industry is vertically structured, so if the top guys take something seriously, then the lower guys take it very seriously. Farmers are horizontal, especially in North Dakota, and must actually know how to do real things. Manure will go only so far for them. We're losing a culture here. The fence lines have been plowed through and the fields are a half mile long and there's no lower forty anymore—it's the lower four hundred. There are a few small farms where thirty or forty Holsteins stand out in the field, but the thousand-head dairy factory is becoming the norm. People who don't have that kind of capital try to scratch out a living making crafts or trading stocks on the Internet or dealing antiques, which there are a lot of in the country. They scrape along; meanwhile, braggarts and bullies rise to power and acclaim. Why, Lord? Meanwhile, the rancid vapors of right-wing radio swirl around us and the tragedy of the war in Iraq. The government is in the hands of people who are lacking a sense of reality. But have courage. All is not lost. This is not the Age of the Hapsburgs, it's America. The people will be pushed just so far. They will tolerate this naked president just so long and then they'll turn their backs on him and walk away.

Meanwhile, I'll have an egg salad sandwich. Cheap at the price: $3.85. I give her a ten and get change and put a five in her tip jar and she sees this. She doesn't smile— she can't be bought—but her eyes soften. Overtipping is allowed. She spreads mayo on the bread and a half cup of egg salad and two leaves of lettuce and slices it on the diagonal and sets it on a plate.

I take a seat at a corner table facing the window. A blustery spring day. The mutter of cars and buses as they pull up to the stop sign. Western Avenue, once the city limit back when little farms lay between St. Paul and the milling city of Minneapolis. On the corner is the old drugstore where F. Scott Fitzgerald came to buy his cigarettes the summer of 1919 when he was living in his parents' garret, a Princeton dropout and failed adman and former lieutenant who never got in the war. He walked down the street, 22, handsome, on the wagon, working up the novel that made him famous, *This Side of Paradise*. Book and author caught the crest of the Jazz Age and swept to fame, romance, terrible celebrity, wealth, happiness, success, insanity, desperation, failure, desperate resolution, vain hope, sudden death, but when he walked down that sidewalk and turned the corner at Selby Avenue, he was just a writer engrossed in the task of trying to turn a loser into a winner. He was born two blocks from here in 1896. His mother had lost two babies and he was the third, and from her lavish love sprouted a boy who believed he could throw the long touchdown pass and win the unattainable girl, be a war hero, and write the Great American Novel.

St. Paul was a provincial outpost to him, a city of shanty Irish and potatoheads, a cold colony he would escape and find his way to Manhattan and Paris and Hollywood and never return here. The land of bitter winds and smug self-effacing people. And yet when Fitzgerald said, "My generation of radicals and breakers-down never found anything to take the place of the old virtues of work and courage and the old graces of courtesy and politeness," he was talking about St. Paul.

When I was still in high school, I walked around this neighborhood and thought about him. It astonished me to read the opening of *Gatsby* and "Winter Dreams" and *The Crack-Up* and think, "The man who wrote this grew up a few blocks from Aunt Jean and Uncle Les's house." When Grandpa rode the streetcar to St. Paul to take out his naturalization papers, the pretty boy in knee pants and swinging his book strap might have been Fitzgerald. Up and down the avenues, past the old brick and stone mansions of the Hills and Griggses and Weyerhausers and Ordways, I anguished in a satisfying way about death, my death, and how nobody ever would know I had the grand ambitions that I had, poor little me, dying unknown, unsung, the tiny obituary (STUDENT SUCCUMBS TO FLU). I used to sit on a little triangle of grass behind a statue of Nathan Hale, his hands tied behind his back, about to be hanged, and watch approaching headlights on Summit Avenue and think, in a satisfying and literary way, about how alone and lost and misunderstood I was. (In fact, was not: was encouraged by many, found good teachers wherever I looked, and had been lucky my whole life.) I looked at a graceful old house and imagined how happy life would be if only I owned it, a brick palazzo with French doors opening onto a terrace from which I could extrapolate a life of affection and amiable conversation. Dark ladies smoking Herbert Tareytons, their long legs draped over a stone balustrade, speaking in low urgent tones about a book, an important book, terribly important, and their expressive hands map out the New World this book foresees in the mist, having torn the roof off the old one. I love the conversation of passionate believers. I was brought up by cautious people who taught me to make haste slowly, and yet I have always wanted more than one life, including some passionate ones—a St. Paul one but also a

New York one, and a cowboy life, of course, and a show-biz one, and a literary one, and a secret life as, say, a singer in a club in Duluth. I lived a lot of lives vicariously as a reader and then invented a few lives of my own. When, at the age of forty, I bought a big green frame house with a porch on Goodrich Avenue, it only made me restless. I pulled up stakes and moved five blocks away to a brick house with a walled garden, then jumped to a belle epoque apartment in Copenhagen where I paced and plotted my escape, then to Central Park West in New York, then to a log cabin in a grove of aspens in Wisconsin with a family of wild turkeys who came and went. And then landed back here in St. Paul, near Nathan Hale, and here I have stopped.

A couple of patrons nod to me and I nod back. I hear my name whispered, and the sound of it triggers a reflex: *you're being watched, try to look intelligent.* I am in that gray eminence stage of life when people take you for someone notable though they don't know what for. "Are you famous?" a girl asked me once; I shook my head. A person doesn't have to be if he doesn't want to. Fame makes you stupid and the writing goes dead and you grab on to the gin bottle. So don't get famous. Line up with the rank and file where the fun is.

Sometimes I feel a hot stare and detect hostility—we Minnesotans don't care to be patronized, as the old *Variety* headline said, STIX NIX HIX PIX, and plenty of Minnesotans are crusty about me and Lake Wobegon, thinking I've hixed them. Nonetheless I am perfectly content here.

When my mother was 15, she lived a few blocks from here with Aunt Jean and Uncle Les. She'd been sent over from Minneapolis by her dad because she had a rebellious streak, went to movies, liked to talk with boys, went to dances. She attended St. Paul Central and studied to be a nurse and after school she went around selling homemade cookies to help pay her way in the world. I think of her, carrying a boxful of bags of cookies along Summit Avenue and screwing up her courage to march to the door and ring the bell. And the lady opens the door and Mother says, "Good afternoon, would you care to purchase a dozen fresh peanut butter cookies?" And a balloon appears over the lady's head: *NO.* And a string of bubbles and another balloon: *There ought to be a law against beggars.* And the door is closed, *whammmm,* and the girl blushes and her heart sinks and she heads toward the next house. A long afternoon on the cookie route.

It's like the beginning of a fairy tale, "The Peanut Butter Cookie Girl," in which she is about to eat all her cookies and perish in a snowbank and then a prince shows up with a crystal slipper in hand. The truth is, my mother would've found a prince like Fitzgerald insufferable. She had the plain good manners of working people who didn't indulge drunkenness and jumping into fountains and self-dramatization in general. My mother can be very sniffy toward rich people and so could Dad. He felt superior to people who spent money to show off. Felt uneasy in fancy houses or around the flamboyant rich. Had no desire to meet the queen. Preferred a Ramada Inn to the Ritz. No Cadillac, thank you. He took pride in modesty and spending money carefully because, after all, you worked hard for it, didn't you?

My 16-ounce Americano with an extra shot of espresso, two biscotti, comes to $4.95. I am 63 and in my mind the value of a cup of coffee is still around 35 cents but I'm willing to pay extra for the pleasure of hanging out with Democrats. I grew up with these folks; they are where my world begins. A civilized people, who enjoy the hubbub of the city, the yawp and jabber of the crowd, the slang and gossip, the old songs and legends, the great bootstrap stories. The ambitious immigrant who puts his kids through college. The person who overcomes a handicap to climb the mountain. The lucky lunch ladies who for fourteen years put a quarter apiece in the pot every payday to buy a lottery ticket and then won—Phyllis, Susan, Judith, Roseanne, Betty, Mary, Alice, Donna, Barbara, Karen, Doreen, Cathy, Elaine, Nancy, and two Kathleens—$95 million, and the next morning went to work and served lunch. The people who persevere. Duke Ellington and his great band barnstorming the segregated South, adored in London and Paris and Copenhagen and they couldn't get a cup of coffee in Georgia or Alabama. The young painters in their low-rent lofts in the Village when New York was the center of the art world. The poets who slept in train stations and sold their blood for lunch money as they summoned up their gift. Dancers subsisting on ramen noodles, actors who walked ten miles to save bus fare, violinists scarfing up leftovers at the country club wedding reception, their big meal of the week, novelists scraping by without health insurance, writing until 3 A.M. month after month with no idea that anything will come of this rigorous life. There's a reason why 95% of people in the arts are Democrats. An artistic gift is dropped on you by God, and if you attend to the gift and are true to it, you will sometimes be in serious need of a helping hand. Art is an imperative stronger than commerce. Republicans don't understand this. They cherish you if you're rich and famous, they can't do enough for you if there's nothing you need, but when you're hard up, don't go to the front door of the manor, go around to the back and the hired help will take you in. And art speaks for the powerless. A poor child in the street is a better choice for a point of view than the tycoon in his study: this we know. Ishmael rather than Ahab; Huck rather than Judge Thatcher. The democracy of American letters is hospitable to outsiders: readers are curious and adventuresome and want to see beyond their own bailiwick and they crave news from the wrong side of town. Artists tend toward an outsider point of view, are drawn toward stories of failure, know that satire is always in behalf of the underdog and the outnumbered, and are committed to the forbidden and dangerous and thrilling thing, namely, the truth. This makes them unwelcome in the Republican Church, which is not (thank you very much) about outsiders or about truth: it is about getting everything you can get and hanging on to it for dear life. It is the party of paranoia, hunkered down, watching for black choppers, obsessed with Big Gummint, which, in any case, under the current occupant, has gotten bigger and bigger and more and more inept.

THE GOOD DEMOCRAT

There was a House Speaker named Hastert
Who went out one night and got plastert
And danced in the nude
And managed to elude
Attention, the lucky old bastert.

1. Democrats distrust privilege and power. Power unchecked runs amok, tears up the grass, and the privileged become sluggish and dull if nobody talks back to them. We think royalty should ride bicycles and carry their own luggage; we think famous people ought to fix their kids' breakfasts and attend their school concerts. The celebrity entourage, the big limo, the luxury suite: signs of self-esteem problems, the urchin complex. We don't like divas who abuse the help, or rock stars who devastate hotel rooms, or CEOs who get big raises when the ship is sinking, or anybody riding high who spits on the peons below. If you earn $14 million a year, you better keep your nose clean and not try to write off your family vacation as a business expense. (Congressman Martin Olav Sabo of Minneapolis authored the Income Equity Act that would deny companies a tax deduction for excessive executive compensation; that is, the portion of the CEO's salary that is more than 25 times the salary of the lowest-paid full-time company employee. If starting pay for the lowliest file clerk is $18,000, then the CEO's salary in excess of $450,000 is not deductible as a business expense. The act has been kept bottled up in the House Ways and Means Committee, a little nod toward democracy that is anathema to some Republicans.)

The most powerful man is a deranged person with a loaded gun who has nothing to lose, and here are we, vulnerable because we have loved ones and a life that is precious to us, and between him and us stands the power of government. I choose not to walk the streets of St. Paul with a pistol in my pocket because it strikes me as slightly demented. Because it's not 1845. Because having one doesn't fascinate me. Because my sympathy is with the cops who have to think about guns every time they walk up to a front door or pull someone over to the side of the road. I count on the civil society to defend me. Defending the powerless against the powerful is a basic task of government, an article of faith in the America I grew up in. Walking into the supermarket, you are powerless to investigate the meatpacker who packaged these Glo Brite wieners so the government must do it for you. The government is there to do battle with those who would sell you cars that are firebombs or TV sets that cause cancer in small children or vitamins that make hair sprout on your palms or hamburgers made from deceased springer spaniels. Every year the bank examiners come around to look at the books and make sure that the president of First Texas Trust isn't siphoning your money to his account in Geneva— How did Republicans manage to make this an issue? Every pickpocket is in favor of deregulating petty theft, every talentless jerk would like to take the onus off plagiarism. Well, think again. *You can't suddenly change the rules to suit yourself. You can't stop the train and kick off the people you don't like. You can't tower over*

people and roar and screech and spray saliva on them.
You can't prey on the preoccupied and slip in a 2% sur-
charge on the electric bill and thereby filch a billion dol-
lars a few cents at a time. You can't sell bad meat or
water the beer or charge 25% interest or piss in the
public water supply. You can't put a quarter in the col-
lection plate and take a dollar out. Democrats thought
that this was understood.

2. Equality is Democratic bedrock. Democrats believe in
writing your own story and putting it up against other
people's on a level court and let the game begin and
more power to you, sing your song and do your dance,
but don't be under the illusion that you invented yourself. Don't be so superior you're offended at the thought
of the progressive income tax. There is an old geezer in
a captain's cap with a hundred buttons pinned to it and
an electric fan suspended from the brim, an orange vest
with badges and flag decals, who rides around the neighborhood from time to time on a three-wheeler with
a fringed green canopy over it and a Bush-Cheney
bumper sticker and a horn and a bell, with a look of royalty and privilege about him as if he were the Duke of

Northumberland accompanied by the Royal Fusiliers, which is okay by me—self-expression is a fine thing—but I look at him and realize why I love the liturgy of the Anglican Church: because I and my friends didn't write it, those are everybody's words. Collective expression is the rare thing; self-expression is common as dandelions. An old Democrat is of course in favor of freedom of self-expression—go tattoo whatever vulgarity you want on your forehead, go sound your barbaric war cry—but this old Democrat prefers the King James and the Lord's Prayer and the old Lutheran table grace (*Be present at our table, Lord; be here and everywhere adored; Thy children bless and grant that we may feast in paradise with Thee*) and all the common treasures from blues to children's rhymes to John Henry and Frankie and Johnny and Jon Jonson of Wisconsin to knock-knock and lightbulb jokes to aphorisms that express the ordinary skepticism of people. We reside in a city of memory and share the avenues with the others. It is a wicked world, in which the power to do harm is so great and the power to do good so slight and an angry fool can do more damage in a day than a hundred wise men can fix in a year, but here we are, we must do our best and do it as a people and when I'm in a crowd singing "America the Beautiful" a cappella I get emotional about the pilgrims' feet and the alabaster cities and the heroes proved in liberating strife, which belong to us all and don't need improvement.

A writer starts out trying to express how thoughtful he is and occasionally brilliant and as he loses interest in that, what sustains him is the love of the common language, English, whose beauty is that it has been enriched from below, by street patois and criminal lingo and teen slang and black English and immigrant languages. Prizes for brilliance are a dime a dozen: what's really special is to write something that speaks for others. To say large things in a small voice.

3. We Democrats are inclusive and integrationist to the core. We cross social barriers and climb through strata. We are fond of cities where classes merge on a daily basis and life bubbles up from below, where high society hangs out with show folks, bankers meet dancers, Lutherans consort with Catholics, Samaritans mill among Judeans, black meets pink and brown, and Jesus moves among the publicans. If we go to Copenhagen, we choose not to stay at the luxury hotel where the staff is careful never to speak Danish in your presence. We prefer to stay with a Danish family so we can eat what they eat for breakfast, watch their TV shows, meet their kids, feel that we've brushed elbows with real life. We think gated communities are creepy, exclusiveness on principle is un-American. The all-male golf club is a charming relic out of P. G. Wodehouse, and God bless the old boys in their knickers with their mashies and niblicks, but leave me out, please. Every time I've found myself in elevated company—sitting on the dais at a dinner, mingling with the thousand-dollar donors—I feel a sad diminution of energy and spark. Irreverence is the engine of wit and you find it in the cheap seats. I'd rather not go to the Middle East or Indonesia where an American travels from one secure compound to another: I'd rather stay home and be a free man than a prisoner of security. The Ritz is the Ritz, a fortress against happenstance, but a person craves street life and a day spent bumping around in Brooklyn or Montmartre or Marylebone Street. Whitman said, "I find letters from God dropped in the street and every one is signed by God's name." God's grace is in the street, among the tourists and the hayshakers. I walk along Wabasha Avenue in St. Paul and a man steps up and asks, "Aren't you Garrison Keillor?" I am, and he sticks out his hand and says, "I've never read your books but I've heard a lot about you." And pauses a beat and says, "You don't suppose you could spare a few bucks for an old bum on the street?" What excellent timing the man has. He grins and touches my arm. He could be a fundraiser for Yale or the Metropolitan Opera, but instead he shares his talent with the general public. So I reach in my pocket and find a bill and it's a twenty, more than I was planning to donate, but I hand it to him, and why not. Genius should be rewarded.

4. *Democrats are city people at heart, even if we're fond of country and small-town life, and dream of retiring to a bee-loud glade, nonetheless the city is the crowning achievement of society.* A farm is a farm but a city is history. The Lord makes counties but cities are built on the love of conversation and the profound industriousness in our natures, the need to hustle and keep busy.

Sit in Bryant Park on 42nd Street in New York, behind the public library, the tulips and irises in bloom beside a plane of grass, people sitting on benches on the sunny side, in a deep box canyon of handsome buildings. A diverse crowd turning their faces up to the sun. A block away is the old *New Yorker* office where James Thurber and E. B. White toiled and Broadway is off to the west and to the east the magnificent reading rooms of the library. Not so long ago, this park was a dump, the haunt of lost souls, a public nuisance, and now it's one of the most graceful places in America. A joy to sit there and contemplate the daily parade.

We St. Paul Democrats cherish the history of our steamboat and railroad town, and the stories of James J. Hill and Archbishop Ireland, the French who settled in Frogtown, the Swedes of Swede Hollow, the Irish, the Mexicans on the West Side. And so we fight against the 16-lane freeways the Republicans want to build to usher themselves swiftly and smoothly from their office towers to their suburban estates. We scrap for neighborhood development money and fight for the branch library, the little park down the street, the cul-de-sac to defeat the speeders.

We are pedestrians. Walking is a cure for the blues and it's the way to look at stuff. St. Paul is a walking city, like New York or San Francisco. You amble down Selby Avenue and check the health of the boulevard trees and listen to the birds tweedling in them, see the brown beer bottles under the hedge, the dog delicately pissing on the tree, see the bees hovering around yellow petals—good news that perhaps we haven't yet poisoned the garden—and you amble farther, your disposition sweetened by a little exertion, you pick up the common parlance and the hum and rattle of the street and other pedestrians, the different shades of faces, odd signature bits of clothing, mannerisms, interesting gaits, manifest attitudes, dramatis personae, snatches of dialogue drifting past ("As if!"), phrases of love and irritation, slang, vagrant obscenities. Benevolent children and their dogs, coffee and pizza smells in the air, the whine of tires, the rumble of buses with enormous portraits of news anchors on the sides all airbrushed and plastic like news anchors in every American city and in the bus windows above their vacant mugs are the Edward Hopper bus riders heading downtown to clean the offices, peddle papers, wash dishes, a busload of patient humanity. And the lovers, faces shining, out for a walk, newly joined, oblivious.

I like to hang out in New York, on the Upper West Side, a sort of national left-wing park and bird sanctuary, and walk up Broadway past the street where George Gershwin wrote *Rhapsody in Blue* and the building Isaac Bashevis Singer lived in when he wrote his tales of Jewish village life in Europe—Holden Caulfield's hotel is nearby where he met the prostitute—and feel in the soles of my feet the vital connection between liberals and cities and artists: the common faith that genius and courage and artistic energy rise up from below and if a nation puts too great burdens on the young and the poor and the dispossessed, if the strata harden, the nation will suffocate its own genius. You don't encourage invention and ambition by giving a quarter-million-dollar tax break to a $15-million-a-year man. Give the bus driver's bright children a chance to get a great education for free. That's an investment. Board the New York City subway in the morning among the young editorial assistants and fledgling security traders; ride in the early evening with violinists and cellists heading for work at Lincoln Center and in the Broadway pits. Walk into the deli and there's Emanuel Ax, one of the greatest pianists on the planet, looking over the cheese selection. Not far away is the neighborhood of Langston Hughes, Allen Ginsberg, Fats Waller, Billie Holiday, Thelonious Monk, and Edward Kennedy "Duke" Ellington, who all came bubbling up from the ranks, and Ellington's great arranger/composer Billy Strayhorn ("Take the 'A' Train," "Lush Life," "After All") who was gay before that was permissible in broad daylight. So many artists flocked to the city of New York because it has always been okay to be gay there. In the 1850s, Walt Whitman traveled freely in the bohemian gay demimonde and behaved flamboyantly for his time and nobody tried to run him out of town, the same Whitman whose "O Captain! My Captain!" was one of my dad's favorite poems. It's a liberal city and it relishes people who are exercising their freedom and having a big time.

It's okay to be an artist or a writer in New York, same as it's okay to be alone. You can eat alone in a café and not feel weird, or the corner deli will sell you half a sandwich and one small brownie. It's okay to talk to yourself in public. Okay to go around on Rollerblades wearing a Donald Duck mask. It's okay to cry in public. No one will think less of you, and people may even offer you some of their medication, or tell you about something going on in their lives that's worse. Same deal in the Democratic Party. Be yourself. Had George W. Bush been a Democrat, he wouldn't have had to deny his colorful past. Cocaine? Tell us about it. Draft dodging? We know about that too. Among Republicans I feel like a rare osprey, stuffed, labeled AUTHOR. Among Democrats I'm not all that different from anybody else.

5. *Democrats believe in individualism.* Social class does not tell the story, nor religion or political party or race or nationality. The important distinctions are between individuals, not between groups. Between two siblings, a vast unbridgeable gulf might exist, whereas between male and female, white and black, straight and gay, Eastern and Western, rich and poor, Democrat and Republican, there is ever the possibility of liaison, friendship, union, miraculous intimacy. People who ought to be enemies are not necessarily. You and I, whoever we are, drifting down the Mississippi on a raft under the stars, fugitives from repression and intolerance, make common cause even though I am Christian and you are something else—this is the spirit I've always found among rank-and-file Democrats. So-called identity politics is punditspeak and nothing important to real Democrats. We believe that individuals are mysterious and elude attempts to categorize them, that all true stories are about individuals and stories purporting to represent Womanhood, Manhood, Jewishness, the African American Experience, Gayness, the South, the Rural Midwest, are fairy tales, sermons, promotional copy. The Great American Story is Huck Finn sticking with the nigger Jim and not betraying him to authorities. The westward migration was away from the class-bound money-dominated East toward the frontier where a friendlier spirit of individualism prevailed and a man was not held in contempt because he was broke or drunk or dressed oddly. (Oscar Wilde was a big hit when he toured the mining camps of the West.) The legends of the Great Depression and Dust Bowl and the Good War are about perseverance but also about grace and generosity between strangers. The friendship of the prince and the pauper. Unlikely friendship is a pure American theme. The strangers in the club car on the Sunset Limited, in the Chatterbox Café on Main Street, and now on the Internet, the great urge to be understood as individuals, not types. In Europe we are thought naive for our rush to be friends and exchange phone numbers and make lunch dates. To a Dane, friendship is no simple matter, but an American leans toward you and starts talking about his childhood, his family, and may tell about his bipolar problem or his AA experience or his sufferings at the hands of his children, and it spurs him on if you are Danish—he insists on trying to leap that gap. The reason for fairness as a political principle is simple: you don't screw people who are, or could be, might soon be, your friends.

6. Democrats are union guys. The spiritual base of the party is the union, that grand Victorian institution that proposes that employees have a say in the workplace and bargain as a group and not be beaten down one by one. The holy martyrs who opened the way to labor unions were those Jewish immigrant women, some of them teenagers, locked by their bosses into the Triangle Shirtwaist Factory in Greenwich Village on March 25, 1911, who, when the fire broke out in the scrap bins, had no escape and leaped to their deaths, 146 of them. Now Wal-Mart is locking its employees into the warehouses at night to discourage pilfering, so not much has changed.

At United Parcel Service, the starting wage for drivers is $8.70 an hour, about what it was thirty years ago, believe it or not. Unions are a good idea unless you are planning to win the lottery. They fight for the skilled jobs that pay $25 an hour or more, enough to enable you to buy a house and have children.

In my line of work, I encounter the American Federation of Musicians, which, among many other things, enforces a few basic work rules so that management (me) can't work musicians overtime without paying overtime. At least, that's the idea. In fact, musicians are as scared as UPS drivers of getting sacked, scared to speak up, to be troublemakers. Classical musicians are in oversupply—three hundred violists might rush to fill one vacancy—and orchestra strikes are rare. These are the people, beautifully trained, neurotic perfectionists, who perform for the carriage trade at the opera and the ballet, who do *Messiah* and *The Nutcracker*, who transport you with the Beethoven *Pastoral* symphony and break your heart with the Mahler Fourth, and in the end they are workers, who worry about pensions and health benefits. Even if you can play that gorgeous French horn solo in Mendelssohn's *A Midsummer Night's Dream*, you still need to pay your kids' dentist.

I met my hero S. J. Perelman once at a dinner and sat across the table from him, stunned with admiration, trying to frame a compliment that would be substantial but not grandiose, and then he leaned over and groused about the *New Yorker* and its miserly treatment of writers, asked me how much they were paying me, shook his head when I told him, said I was worth more than that, said it was a battle he'd been fighting all his life, this assumption on the part of management that we were all goddamned Du Ponts, and this brotherly conversation, like a couple of metalworkers grousing over lunch, endeared him to me forever. To be regarded as a fellow worker by S. J. Perelman meant more to me than any prize.

Unions are a little fence against sadism. You can't, even if you're a genius with wild hair and a long baton, keep the orchestra rehearsing through their scheduled break. Even if you're tuned to the universal harmony of the spheres, people still have the right to pee. Even if you come to the end of rehearsal and only need five more minutes, you can't have them without paying for fifteen or thirty, whatever the contract says. So geniuses learn to watch the clock and plan their time. The union is a conservative force, resists change, is wary of innovation, and that can be maddening (though the same can be said of the National Association of Broadcasters or the American Medical Association, both of them on the trailing edge of progress), but the union seeks to protect the dignity of its people, and that is its nobility. Without the union, they'd be treated like Holsteins; with it, they can moo at you and if you want to fire them, you have to follow procedure. You can't just shoot them in the knees.

7. A Democrat begins with sympathy for the helpless, especially children and the elderly. Sympathy is the barometer of our humanity; to the extent that we share each other's griefs and joys, we are fully alive. A person so trapped in his own head and obsessed with his own minutiae that news of earthquakes, hurricanes, drought, genocide, terror, ships sinking, trains derailing has little meaning to him, is cut off, a man without a species. He reads the story about the family who burned up in their shack, from the explosion of a kerosene stove, but it happened three miles away, no concern of his. He hears a child shriek outside but he has no children so he doesn't go to the window. From here, it is not far to the villagers going about their business downwind from the ovens of Auschwitz. We Democrats are not nannies and our interest in, say, putting helmets on bikers or making people use inclusive pronouns is vastly less than in saving innocent children from lead poisoning, the half-million toddlers in poor neighborhoods who ingest paint chips and dust and suffer brain damage, thanks to the carelessness of adults. You see welfare parents with their children and sometimes you want to grab the parents and shake them, they are so clueless and foulmouthed and cruel, but you can't, so you hope that the social workers in Child Protection have enough funding to keep up with their caseload.

Sympathy is a basic creaturely trait, the vibration of one's being at the cry of another human—the old lady with swollen feet who clambers aboard the jam-packed bus, the woman struggling toward the gate at the airport holding one infant and pushing another in a stroller and hauling two carry-on bags, the old man climbing over the icy snowbank on the corner, the abused child, the wounded hero languishing in red tape, the old doo-wop singer cheated by the big recording label, the man on death row unfairly accused and railroaded through—your heart goes twang, and you offer a hand. If you don't, then I will; if neither of us does, then someone will. This is the measure of a decent community: we refuse to watch suffering and turn away.

I grew up reading *Black Beauty* and *Heidi* and *Hans Brinker, or the Silver Skates* and other books about abused underdogs redeemed in the end, which excited my pity, a strong emotion in a child. When the good horse was mercilessly beaten, I wept and could hardly read more. Now, if I sit passively and let the old lady stand clinging to a strap and don't offer my seat as the bus pulls away, I am deeply ashamed. The damage done to children in East Harlem is a shame to the patrons of the opera and the ladies and gentlemen dining at La Grenouille and so we embrace the idea of the safety net that catches the fallen, for which the wealthy pay a heavier share, because most Americans aren't willing to see shantytowns spring up outside town or have crowds of hollow-eyed children trailing us in the streets, keening and begging. Most Americans are not willing to let people die in a ditch or go hungry. Democrats aren't, that's for sure.

People are responsible for the dumb things they do, yes indeed. There is a Moment of Reckoning that comes occasionally to each one of us and we're entitled to it. The truth dawns. If you leave your bike outside, it will rust. If you build on a floodplain, eventually you will get flooded out and your sofa will be waterlogged and your linoleum come loose. If you're worried about drinking, stop. If you smoke cigarettes, you may wind up with lung cancer or emphysema. If you gamble, you may lose your shirt.

There are, however, broken people in this world and it does not help matters to order them to shape up and then walk away. You wouldn't do that with anyone you knew personally. Other people count, even broken ones. You cannot gallop through the streets like a Cossack and not notice who you are tromping into the dirt, who curses you as you go jangling past. You cannot do this in life, in business, or in politics, wielding power in behalf of your cronies in the American Petroleum Party—you really cannot—there will come a Day of Reckoning. You learn this when you're two years old and other little kids climb into the sandbox with you: the sand must be shared. Jesus said, "Unless ye become as little children, ye cannot enter into the kingdom of heaven."

8. Democrats are die-hard teachers. Education is a heroic task and the answer to just about anything. The Peace Corps was pure Democratic idealism: send diligent young pedagogues out into the ramshackle parts of the world to teach hygiene and reading and corn planting and well digging and you will cast bread upon the waters and accomplish endless good. Offer college courses to prison inmates and you will raise morale and reduce violence in ways that lockdowns cannot. Sit the drug addicts down in a circle and get them to educate each other. Even violent young adolescent males can be rescued by the right sort of teacher. Education is an expensive proposition but there's no choice: nobody is born smart and we need good schools. Every child needs a beloved teacher in the early grades to instill a love of school, that enchanted world of books and paper and pencils and multiplication tables and maps and pictures, a love that will see the child through stretches of tedium and moments of panic. Every child needs teachers to idolize and imitate and around the snarly age of 14, when our daughters look at us with pained amusement and our sons with loathing, they need teachers who can channel their anger into social criticism and turn them into crusaders and satirists, as we once were, and then they will have children of their own and become us, the tedious authoritarians, and we will become beloved and eccentric grandparents, the genial revolutionaries, working secretly with our grandchildren against our common enemy, the parents. This is how the world turns. And teachers are crucial.

When you wage war on the public schools, you're attacking the mortar that holds the community together. You're not a conservative, you're a vandal. The sorehead vote is out there, the guys who have a few beers and wonder why the hell they should have to pay taxes for the schools when their kids have graduated—What's the logic there, Joe?—and you can rouse them up and elect a school board to take revenge on the teachers and you do your community no favors.

Redneck used to refer to farmers like my uncle Jim who did indeed have a red neck and forearms and face right up to the cap line on his forehead, but he was a generous sweet-tempered Christian man who lived out his faith. Now *redneck* just means somebody who'd happily spend $40,000 on a new pickup for himself and rise up in rage if someone asked him to pay $200 more for his kids' education. They're not farmers, they're just selfish bastards with shit for brains who only pay attention to education when they get pissed off. The school board, a dedicated bunch of hardworking individuals, decides to change the school nickname from the Redskins to the Hornets, and the word goes out to the tavern dwellers and for the next school board meeting the gymnasium is packed with furious large men venting their lifelong frustrations and in the fall the school board is thrown out of office and replaced by angry large people. That's redneck politics. The new school board sets about restoring Redskins honor, and trimming the budget, cutting out French and Spanish, establishing creationism as the prevailing science, cleansing the library of impurities, teaching faith-based social studies and history. High school becomes a forced hike down a long corridor of locked doors. You earmark your children for careers as drones—no need for them to learn a second language or write poetry or study physics: in a good redneck school, they only need to learn to sit quietly and recite the official line and become angry rednecks like their daddies.

9. Democrats are realists. We care less about symbolism and enacting our own theology into law and making people listen to us intone a prayer (*O Thou who didst reveal Thyself to us, grant us victory over our despicable foes, and rain destruction and despair on them and cover their bodies with boils and sores, we do earnestly seek this in Our Savior's Name—amen*) and we care more about the ordinary essentials of life. The New Deal put real people to work. My uncle Don was 18 in Wausau, Wisconsin, a big red-haired football star with no prospects, and got a job with the Civilian Conservation Corps and went off to build paths in national parks, a big experience for him. The Rural Electrification Act extended electric power to farms and villages that couldn't afford the capital investment: good old American socialism. The Keillor farm was one. They wired the barn so Uncle Jim had steady light to milk the cows by on winter mornings and a fluorescent light in the kitchen so he could read the Bible at night. Democrats brought about the school lunch program and the Public Health Service and integrated the armed forces, which then became a model of how Americans can be not so hung up on race. Democrats produced Head Start and food stamps and funded the college buildings to house the wave of boomers in the Seventies. The goal of Democrats has been to make this a nation of the middle class—educated people who own property and have a stake in the community and aren't easily bullied—and the most dramatic program was the GI Bill of Rights, which boosted a whole generation into the ranks of white-collar professionals.

We are all, God bless us, uniquely ordinary and rise up in the morning and wash our faces and pull our pants on, and it would be nice to eat a breakfast that isn't full of poisons, send our children off to a good school, ride a safe bus to work at a building that complies with health laws, and use a cell phone that won't give us brain cancer. We'd like our employer to treat us fairly according to accepted practice. We'd like the police to guard the city against predators and vandals. We'd like to imagine that city officials are visionary and honest and committed to the common good and not in the pocket of the power company. We'd like to think that people in trouble get rescued. This is the Democratic view. We prefer the secular society to one in which persons of unpopular beliefs are ostracized, and we don't make the American flag into the Shroud of Turin, and we refuse to be cowed by our own government, and the sexual lives of our neighbors are not of profound interest. Republicans are troubled by homosexuality and can't figure out how not to think about it. Hunger and homelessness don't get their attention but the sight of two women kissing gets Republicans all buzzed, what a porch light does for moths. Democrats care more about health care and other staples of middle-class life. You drive out of St. Paul into the Republican suburbs and you see what the New Deal and Fair Deal and Great Society accomplished: they enabled people of modest means to get a leg up in the world and eventually become right-wing reactionaries and pretend that they sprang fully formed from their own ambitions with no help from anybody. And vote to deny to others what they themselves were freely given. Bless their hearts, they are some of the meanest folks you'd ever want not to live next to, and their legacy will be a rat's nest of problems.

10. *The values of Democrats are rooted in courtesy and kindness.* Everyone gets knocked around and failure is endemic and some get dealt a lousy hand and yet what gets us through the woods is the grace of God and the kindness of others, their small good deeds, unbidden, milk and honey. The American Indian didn't see much of our kindness, nor African Americans trying to pull themselves up out of sharecropper poverty, but for all our failings, there is a powerful river of mercy and understanding running through this nation's history and Democrats are in that stream.

Let not the sun set upon your wrath. Be grateful for your gifts. Say good morning. Let the customer have his say. Let aggravation pass without response. Yield to the car trying to cut in front of you. Float along in your unclouded brain and enjoy the passing parade. This is an old Democrat's advice.

Liberalism is the politics of kindness. It is all about opening the castle and letting the air in. Joseph McCarthy and the Red hunters of the Fifties were a visceral issue for liberals. Tailgunner Joe was an out-and-out bully and drunkard and liar who operated by innuendo and natural gas, a classic Republican prosecutor-politician, and he and his cohorts came afoul of a deep-seated American aversion to seeing people hauled up before a government committee to be grilled about their beliefs. We have the same aversion to homophobes: it's simply another form of cruelty. So 10 or 12 million people get the vapors if they see two men with earrings holding hands. So what? No need to amend the Constitution to forbid same-sex hand-holding. Let it be.

Sanctity of marriage? Your marriage is between you and your spouse and its sanctity depends on the two of you. You can't beat each other and you can't cheat on each other, without the other having legal recourse, and otherwise you do not require state supervision. If the president wants to defend the sanctity of marriage, why not an amendment banning divorce?

Marriage in the United States shall consist only of the union of a man and a woman, or, in Utah, women. Neither this Constitution or the constitution of any state, nor state or federal law, shall be construed to permit divorce, except if the wife be found to have lost her virginity prior to marriage, in which case she shall be stoned. May not be applicable in Texas.

Gay marriage is an arguable issue and it will be argued. Some of us don't know what we think about it because it doesn't touch us directly. We claim the right to be undecided. When Hallmark starts making cards for gay weddings, then we'll make up our minds.

> *Congratulations as you enter*
> *Marriage to one of your own gender.*
> *May the bells ring loud and gay*
> *On your joyful wedding day.*

I do think that if Larry loves Bruce and they go to the Church of the Blessed Whatever and the Reverend Starflower Moonbright intones some high-flown sentences and turns around three times and clicks his red slippers and proclaims them husband and husband, then I will wish them well and bring them a stainless-steel serving tray wrapped in nice silvery paper with a bow. This is the United States of America in the 21st century. It isn't Ireland, 1928. It isn't Iran. Odd and interesting things happen here. We should know this by now.

When I think of kindness, I think of my aunts, who looked out for neglected kids—runts and orphans and odd ducks, their specialty—and bestowed favors on them.

They extended themselves to strangers. Their hearts went out to the lonely and the grieving. They did not let shyness get in the way of charity. They did not permit bullies to tromp around unimpeded; they spoke up. They abhorred cruelty. It offended them deeply. I don't suppose they would've "approved" of gay marriage but what if their nephew Larry and his partner Bruce were being shunned by some in the family and hounded by others and they had been met at the end of the driveway by Uncle Rex who told them to come no farther, the family Thanksgiving dinner was not open to them? What would my aunts have done? I suspect that one or two of them would've broken ranks and gotten in a car and chased down the prodigals and told them to come back and have some fatted turkey. That spirit runs deep in this country, I do believe. Great empires rise and fall, the famous come and go, cities boom and then languish, but human kindness is a constant presence in America.

Chapter 12

REPUBLICANS
I HAVE KNOWN

A horse-faced Republican, Frist,
Went to a bar and got pissed
And smoked six cigarettes
And was full of regrets
For the profligate youth he had missed.

I N THE fourth grade, I pored over a delicious book, *Runaway Home* by Elizabeth Coatsworth, about a family that moves from Maine to Washington State, traveling in a house trailer and having adventures along the way. I daydreamed that my family and I were nomads, migrating according to whim, camping in beautiful places and then moving on. (I think my dad had the same daydream.) I spent whole afternoons on the bank of the Mississippi, looking at the water flowing over the

219

rapids, imagining myself on a boat heading downstream. I still think about it, standing on the landing in St. Paul and looking at the big curve of the river below downtown. I still love driving to the airport to get on a plane to wherever *A Prairie Home Companion* is playing that weekend. People tell me, "That must be hard on you, all that traveling," but it really isn't. You buckle up and rise to the skies and look at the patchwork quilt of farms pass beneath and feel loosened from the struggle of daily life.

The problem for a writer is that liberation from the struggle is tedious to write about: struggle is material for a writer and ease and comfort are not. And at 37,000 feet, a person starts to think like a Republican.

I didn't want to write this book. A writer resists marching under a banner. A writer doesn't want to be thought of as a loyal Democrat. (Gene McCarthy said, "One thing about a pig, he thinks he's warm if his nose is warm. I saw a bunch of pigs one time that had frozen together in a rosette, each one's nose tucked under the rump of the one in front. We have a lot of pigs in politics." This is the sort of death writers hope to avoid.) Writing is so risky to start with—you might spend three years pecking away at a book and accomplish no more than if you had sat watching TV and eating Cheez-Its— so you cherish your freedom, the thing that makes writing fun, the chance to irritate and enrage. I told my students in the Composition of Comedy course at the University of Minnesota that, old-fashioned as I am, I would not be their censor and they were delighted to test me with a barrage of raunch and scatology and profanity that I must say I found refreshing. They used the f-word brilliantly at times, a little twang on the bottom string. Reading them, you could suddenly understand why newspapers are dying all over America—they are written for prim people in their sixties, people like me! The Internet is the medium of free speech for people under 40 and the beloved old gazette is so encrusted with prohibitions and dead custom that young people are embarrassed to be seen with it in their hands. The newspaper has become a relic like the Moose Lodge because it refuses to be free. It's written by people who are trying to impress their old civics teacher who is long dead and buried. The permanent problem of a writer: to be free. I wrote a newspaper column once in praise of military people I'd met and proposing a constitutional amendment to require the president to be a native-born citizen and a veteran of the armed services, and this alarmed some lefty friends. Once I spoke at a teachers' convention and told the story of why I pulled my son out of public school in the second grade years ago and why I send my daughter to a Christian school today and the crowd got very very quiet. A writer cherishes these moments, when you speak some truth to people leaning the other way.

Early in my career, I wrote stories for the *New Yorker* while my wife and son and I lived in a rented house on a farm in Stearns County. I worked in a tiny bedroom on an Underwood typewriter on a desk made of ¾-inch plywood set across two old filing cabinets, sat and tapped away for hours on yellow copy paper, the farmyard and red barn and silo in the background, half of my brain tuned to that grandly casual *We were strolling along West 43rd the other morning and happened to glance up at the Town Hall marquee* style that I loved, queer as it is, and the other half tuned to the voices of my aunts and uncles, straight dry Midwestern speech. Now I tell stories on the radio about Lake Wobegon and its God-fearing egalitarian inhabitants, and of course I speak with a certain nostalgia, a retrospective love: Life can be brutal and in the face of it, one thinks back to Main Street, Anoka, 1956, and sitting in the office of the Anoka *Herald* writing up sports on a typewriter, the Linotypes clattering in the back room, and watching people I knew go in and out of the Anoka Dairy with ice cream cones on a warm September day—how preposterously beautiful it seems now—which radio listeners seem to enjoy, and though I find grandeur in this, I feel that, at 63, I am still in search of what I was looking for when I was 18. The truth about things. Why am I here? Why did Grandpa and Grandma Denham come over from Glasgow in 1906 with their six kids, Marion, Mary, Ruby, Margaret, Jean, and Bill, and settle into the big frame house on Longfellow Avenue? Grandpa was a railroad clerk who wore hightop black shoes and white shirts with silk armbands and spoke with a Scottish burr, so that girls came out "gettles." He never drove a car or attended a movie or read a novel. I want to know why they came, what they were looking for.

My mother, at age 91, has just told us a story we never heard before. Her best friend at Roosevelt High School was a black girl and they walked home together and told each other everything. That girl was the only one who wanted to be friends with my mother. We want to know more.

The terrible longing to know more, especially now that the historians of our family have died and taken their secrets with them.

But some things I do know about my family and people, their fundamental decency, and that compels me to write a book and raise a voice against this arrogant and dishonest and vicious government.

I have liked plenty of Republicans. Chet Atkins was a Republican, as most people in east Tennessee were, the part of the state that stayed loyal to the Union, and one of the finest human beings I ever met, a gentleman and artist and storyteller and a man with a true gift for friendship. I loved Chet, as so many people did, and there on his office wall hung pictures of him with Reagan, Bush the First, Lamar Alexander, everybody grinning. Reagan has just told a story and Chet is laughing. Senator Dave Durenberger of Minnesota sat in a tea shop in St. Paul with me and talked for almost an hour about his travels in Africa and the people he's met there over the years. Long ago, when the National Endow-

ment for the Arts was under attack over the Map-
plethorpe pictures of naked men with things stuck in
their orifices, I walked into the office of Senator Alan
Simpson, the Republican whip, to make a case for the
NEA and he couldn't wait to tell me about a game
played by Wyoming cowboys in which you drop your
trousers and try to pick up a quarter on a wooden bench
using only your cheeks. A fine gentleman. Justice Harry
Blackmun was a Republican of the old school, and showed
me a framed photograph of himself and the rest of the
Harvard Glee Club posing on the White House lawn
with President Hoover. And a framed bullet that somebody shot through the window of his home, payment
perhaps for his having written the majority opinion in
Roe v. Wade. Every day, this modest man went for a
walk after lunch at his office. He declined to take a security man along with him and followed the same route
every day, returning to the Supreme Court building by
the front entrance, often passing through a crowd of
antiabortion picketers holding up pictures of dead em-
bryos and not recognizing the slight bespectacled man
in the overcoat who had done the devil's work.

I met President Reagan once back in 1991 with

my stepdaughter, a film student at Columbia. Myself, I wouldn't know how to get an appointment with the mayor of Piscacadawadaquoddymoggin but the *New York Times* has clout and an editor there arranged it, hoping I'd write something sharp and satiric about the old man. We went to the top floor of a building in Century Plaza with a view of West LA and the ocean and in he came, beaming, though he hadn't a clue who we were or why we'd come. Had we had trouble finding the address? No. Were we enjoying LA? Yes. Had we visited the Reagan library? No. "But we got to see the old Warner Brothers lot," Malene said. And that lit up the old man's eyes. He turned and bestowed his full sunny warmth on her. Nothing, it seemed to me, not a battalion of Young Republicans or a gold plaque from the National Rifle Association could have warmed his heart as a beautiful young woman who felt (she really did) that the Thirties were the heyday of moviemaking and who revered motion pictures starring old pals of his, and he got all twinkly and Irish. No wonder he got elected despite his tentative grasp of reality and was let off so easily for the Iran-Contra business, an impeachable offense if there ever was one.

I'd enjoy writing that book. I'd write about George Plimpton, a good man and a friend of the Bushes, and I'd try to appreciate their world and see them as graceful, thoughtful, well-meaning people. But the book would crash up against a plain fact: my life depends on the social compact that Republicans are determined to overthrow, cutting taxes and killing off public services and reducing us to a low-wage no-services plantation economy run by an enclave class that I do not wish to be part of, no matter how graceful or thoughtful they are. I don't want to move to a suburban paradise with a guardhouse at the entrance and a private security force. I want to stay here in St. Paul where anyone can walk up to my front door, Jehovah's Witnesses or Boy Scouts selling Christmas wreaths or candidates for city council or firewood salesmen or cat burglars casing the joint, and I want the freedom to walk the streets and enjoy the civility of the city. The Republicans are destroying the neighborhood. When the coyotes become bold, then in defense of small children you must go and deal with coyotes, whether you want to or not.

The irresponsibility of Republicans stems from the coalition of the corporate Bourbon wing of the party and the Bible wing, two groups with almost nothing in common. The Bible wing supplies the votes and the Bourbons run the show. The Bourbons get tax cuts and deregulation and thousands of small favors; the Biblists get massaged on symbolic issues such as gay marriage, abortion, and school prayer. Like the Pharisees, the Biblists enjoy public displays of religion. A roomful of movers and shakers gathered for a prayer breakfast that is all about bonding, backslapping, hobnobbing, and the prayers are read off 3 x 5 index cards, and there is no heartfelt witnessing as you'd find among people of true faith. At the prayer breakfast, if the Holy Spirit speaks, it is always in favor of tax cuts and less government regulation and preemptive military action. The Holy Spirit never comes out in favor of anything without clearing it with the Republican Party.

The Biblists vow to put God back in the public schools, as if He were a small plaster icon and not the Creator of the universe. Evidently, when they hear public prayer, they sense the Spirit's presence. I don't. The public invocation *(O Thou Who didst turn water into wine, bless, we beseech Thee, this conference of the Water Sanitation Engineers of the North Central District . . .)* is a piece of sanctimonious claptrap with the spiritual weight of a postage stamp. It has no connection to true prayer, the throwing of myself down in the presence of the Creator: *Lord have mercy, Lamb of God who takes away the sins of the world have mercy upon us. Our Father Who art in heaven, hallowed be Thy Name.* Saying the names of loved ones, putting myself wordlessly under God's wing. That is true prayer. Pharisee prayer is simply a political speech that is addressed to God, as if He needed instruction. Why are the Pharisees so willing to exploit the Christian faith for political mileage? They will have to answer that; I can't. But God is not mocked. God looks at the reality, and that is disastrous. The waste of young lives in favor of greater privilege for the privileged. (Where did Jesus tell us to do that?)

Faith is private. It demonstrates itself in good works and love of neighbors but it doesn't need to hire a publicist. You're not angling for Christian of the Year and the cover of *Believer* magazine. Your job is to endure the rampages of the heart and to look in your own heart and ask, Do I really believe or do I not? Jews do this in the fall and Christians in early spring, during Lent. Most people do not believe. They have tried to believe and they wish they did believe and are sorry they don't, because they like to be around people who do, so they come to church, and enjoy the music and candles and the hallowedness of it all, but the faith is not in them. They don't need to tell me about it—they only need to answer to God on this matter. He will understand if the answer is no. He already knew that.

Confession is at the heart of the faith (*All have sinned and come short of the glory of God*), but Republicans have revised the faith to remove the stuff about the poor and omit the confession of sin. To them, prayer is a promotional device in which you thank God for making you the true-blue person and 100% patriot that you are. In the Christian view of the world, these folks rank lower than outright atheists—*Better never to have believed than to use sacred things for your grimy self-aggrandizement*—which would scare them if they stopped to think about it.

My parents said grace before every meal, with the plaster Brethren plaques on the wall—JESUS NEVER FAILS, and PRAYER CHANGES THINGS—and faithfully attended the breaking of bread on Sunday mornings and gospel meetings on Sunday nights and Bible readings

on Wednesdays and patiently awaited the Rapture. The
Brethren were gentle dissenters devoted to the Lord's
Word who believed in separation from the things of the
world. You shouldn't make big plans or think too highly
of yourself or curry the favor of nonbelievers or devote
yourself to gathering wealth. They were deeply suspicious of earthly success. On Sunday morning you sat in
the Brethren meeting hall, which was plain, unadorned,
with no pictures or statues or gold or expensive things
because the Brethren lived by the Word and didn't parade their Christian faith for effect. My father thought
the baccalaureate "service" at the high school was silly
on the face of it, mere religiosity, an attempt by the indifferent to play at religious ritual and thereby assuage
their guilty conscience. And that's the Republican Party:
its Christianity is about half fake because it scorns Jesus's
command to love thy neighbor as thyself and it abuses
any who take the commandment seriously. Better to be
a principled atheist than a Christian for show. A man
who employs the Lord as a special effect and makes a
public performance of piety deadens his spiritual life
and puts his own soul in danger.

America is not a religious country, no matter how

many Americans say they believe in God. I've been in religious countries and this is not one of them. There is no Sabbath here, no fasting or prohibitions, every day is a feast day. You can buy liquor on Sunday almost anywhere, find pornography in any Marriott or Wal-Mart, say any ugly, profane thing on the radio or anywhere—we're fat and sloppy and as disciplined as a battalion of cats, an impulsive, dreamy people walking around eating ice cream cones and eyeballing the girls' sweaters and dreaming of a big hit in the lottery. If God is looking for a nation to carry out His will on earth, it isn't this one. And it wasn't leftist professors who led us into the sins of the flesh: it was capitalist entrepreneurs. If the Pharisees really want to make this a God-fearing nation, they should take up their cudgels against the Bourbon wing of the party.

Chapter 13

※○○○○○○○○ ✿ ○○○○○○○○※

ARROGANCE

A progressive named Robert LaFollette
Said, "Taxation is what we call it.
Them what has got
Pays for them what has not
So shut up and pull out your wallet."

DEMOCRATS are said to be weak on foreign policy—
too anxious about world opinion—fearful of the
use of American power in the world—but what we fear
is arrogance. History shows so clearly the stupidities of
1915—old men in power with little notion of where
they were headed, afraid to betray uncertainty or fear,
willing to sacrifice a generation of young men so that
old men could parade around in their plumed helmets
for a few more years—which was also the stupidity of

Vietnam and is still with us today. Great harm has been done by right-wing ideologues who, with supreme self-confidence, forged a doctrine for lands they were beautifully ignorant of and sent young Americans to die for it, just as in 1915 strategists and theoreticians drew lines on a map and sent real soldiers slogging through mud and mist toward impenetrable barriers that on the map didn't appear so. The strategists draw the lines and issue the orders and have lunch in the officers' mess under the chandeliers, and the soldiers move out into the rain and die in the desolate dark.

For my generation of college kids, arrogance was ignorance. Foreign travel was a test of one's character and intelligence. You didn't zoom around Europe in a star-spangled USA NO. 1 jacket waving fistfuls of dollars and speaking in boldface capital letters. We grew up curious about the big world and hoped to really experience it and not an Americanized version, to see villages with no Coca-Cola signs. We worked at marshaling a little French, some Italian, some German, as our humble offering to the natives so they might accept us. We dreaded the stereotype of the ugly American.

When I lived in Denmark in the late Eighties, I went

to parties and listened to the dinner speeches and songs and when the Dane sitting next to me asked, "Shall we speak English or Danish?" I said, "Dansk, naturligvis. Vi er i danmark." And off I went down the slippery slopes. The Dane might be a reader of Updike and Cheever, but I chugged along in my patchy Danish, little shattered sentences stuck together with lumpy participles, because I wanted to get far away from arrogance and also because it's a unique pleasure to express your patriotism in a foreign tongue. You chatter in Danish about New York City and LA and New Orleans, the magnificent West, Chicago, the redwoods, the Grand Canyon, all that Danes love about America, the mythological landscape of books and music. It isn't our politicians they admire, that's for sure.

When I lived there, Danes were still talking about the visit of Vice President Bush to speak at the Danish Fourth of July at Rebild Park in Jutland and how his armor-plated limousine had sunk down in the sand en route to the speaker's pavilion and how the man refused to get out of the damn car and walk 200 yards to the stage. He sat in his behemoth car with Old Glory flying from the front fender, surrounded by Secret Service, and it took twenty men on a hot day to push him through the sand to the pavilion where he disembarked and gave his speech on Freedom, America's Gift to the World. Denmark is a country where big shots walk. Mr. Bush made an impression on the Danes.

He was president when I went to the Danish Fourth of July celebration in 1992 and the day before to a reception at the American ambassador's residence in Charlottenlund, a mansion with a swimming pool in back and a lawn big enough to play softball on. Fifty guests mingled in the sunshine, Danes from the ministry of education and various exchange programs and some Americans from the embassy and a couple of Fulbrighters, and then suddenly the ambassador appeared, a beefy Republican with a big honk that made you flinch and look away, embarrassed that your country was represented by such a yahoo. He circulated through the crowd, grabbing people's shoulders ("Hey, how we doin' here? Need a refill?"), the perfect caricature of the self-made tycoon ("You want another beer? Hey! Go for it!"). This man represented the defeat of American satire. Mark Twain, H. L. Mencken, George Ade, Sinclair

Lewis, and James Thurber had all beaten on this man for a hundred years and there wasn't a dent in him. He stood there, drink in hand, as fresh and happy and stupid as if *Babbitt* had never been written. He read his speech off a sheet of paper, bellowing into a microphone. "Velkommen and Tak," he said. "And now I think I'll switch to English. Danish always sounds to me like someone choking on a potato." He paused for the laugh, not understanding that it's only funny if a Dane makes fun of Danish: coming from an American, it's rude. He read his little talk about the Fulbright program, said it was a good thing and he was in favor of it and stepped down, a Republican through and through—crass, smug, contemptuous of foreigners, inept at English, anti-intellectual and damn proud of it, a Busher all the way. At his elbow, prompting him, doing damage control, a career Foreign Service officer, one of those modest, diligent people who bother to do their homework and get the lay of the land. Meanwhile, the bozo went hollering through the crowd—and he got away with it because Danes admire America. Not for people like him but for jazz musicians, artists, writers, and of course for the GIs who helped rescue Europe from the Nazis. He was a man writing a check on other people's accounts.

We Democrats do not want to be him. We prefer Adams and Franklin and Jefferson, who made the voyage across the Atlantic and polished their French and learned to make their way by their wits and not by throwing money around or at the point of a cannon. America has produced great travelers and explorers and missionaries. They didn't stand behind a podium and thunder and threaten and strike a belligerent pose to impress the folks in Topeka, they went out into the world with courage and curiosity to take it on its own terms. They looked, they listened, they learned to walk lightly. The young Bill Clinton rambled around Europe with a knapsack and a train pass, getting the ground view, meeting ordinary people, living on the cheap. It was a big experience for a young man from Arkansas. The young George W. never considered foreign travel until he was able to have a motorcade and be sheltered from all natural interaction with aliens.

Chapter 14

9/11

A Republican lady of Knoxville
Bought her brassieres by the boxful,
Which she stuffed with corn kernels
And old Wall Street Journals
To keep the fronts of her frocks full.

I T HAS RAINED all morning on Republican and Democrat alike and at noon I go to the café. A soft and glittery world after rain. The urge to strive and accomplish and succeed relaxes on a rainy day. The chain gang is canceled, public hangings postponed. It's the day to savor the goodness of life. Once the water collects in rivers, men can fight over it and apportion it away from the gardens of the poor and lavish it on the fairways of the rich, but for now, it is simple socialism in the form of precipitation. Our neighbors' yard glistens, the dark brown patches where their three boys and our daughter have worn holes in the turf, scuffling around the swing set. I walk past Jim and Debra's house and the old Field house and turn the corner. A little girl died here three years ago. For weeks afterward, little bouquets of flowers were laid on the boulevard. There are tragedies that nobody can rescue you from. A thoughtless moment compounded by happenstance and a child is killed and you spend the rest of your life looking at the X and wondering why did it happen like that when it could have happened so many other ways. And on this same corner I once saw a bride and groom, just the two of them, in white and black, cross the street under an umbrella, heading for their reception at the University Club, in a downpour, he holding her hand up and forward, as if leading her in a dance.

I sit and drink coffee in the corner café on Selby and remember the Ten O'Clock Scholar near the U where I hung out forty years ago. Fishnet hung from the ceiling and candles burned in Chianti bottles on tables that were wooden telephone-cable spools and silent men played chess in the corner and sometimes a chick with a

Swedish last name would sing the blues, *I'm going to town to get my ashes hauled because my good man he left me in the fall,* and I sat in back, studying people, reading their clothing, trying to distinguish the nobodies like me, the blue-collar kids from Coon Rapids and Fridley, from the chic and shameless from the horsey suburbs of Wayzata or North Oaks. O the pleasures of reverse snobbery! The student art on the walls was all browns, ochre, black wash, shadowy, ominous, lonely figures, woodcuts, storm clouds, dark houses. Dark was cool and to be anguished meant you were serious. I could be dark with the best of them.

I think if I sat here long enough, I might see my 18-year-old self walk in the door. He'd stand by the cash register and scan the room and his gaze would be merciless. I dread him looking at me. Here I am, walking softly through my sixties, one more earnest Midwesterner, a little astonished at my good fortune in life; when I was 18, I was poised on the crest of the hill, about to plunge down the slippery slope to a lifetime of failure. Nine years later, an unsolicited story of mine was bought by the *New Yorker* magazine and this stroke of good luck began to reverberate in my life. The *New*

Yorker was a name that rang loud and long in the minds of Midwesterners, and my association with the magazine was a powerful juju. I wrote a story for the *New Yorker* about the radio show *The Grand Ole Opry* at WSM in Nashville and that opened the door to my starting *A Prairie Home Companion* in 1974. No commercial station would've been interested, and the classical music stations of public radio wouldn't have been either, but there was that interesting item in my résumé, my connection to the *New Yorker*, and that juju opened doors. It helped that my boss, William H. Kling, was fond of antique radio and of course it helped that I worked hard (which one must do if one is not naturally gifted—as Grandma said, "What we lack in our heads, we must make up for with our feet") but looking back, I see that the *New Yorker*'s acceptance letter in the spring of 1969 was a magical coin dropped on my doorstep. So much happened to me as a result of that one thing— an anonymous *New Yorker* underling, some Smith or Wellesley girl, interning for the summer, riffling through crates of stuff, came across my little story and snatched it up in her hand—and had she not, I'd be driving the

Grand Avenue bus or waiting tables at the Lexington Café. I ponder this on a more or less daily basis.

The radio show is a job, but one I do by reflex, so it doesn't depend on ambition or initiative or creativity. The Great Listener is standing over me, holding an old tennis ball, and as I look up at Him, panting, He throws the ball into the bushes and I tear after it and bring it back. I do that every week, over and over. I'm not a performer by nature. I suffer over it as much as my mother dreaded knocking on doors to sell cookies, but I am a lucky man. It goes back to that Smith or Wellesley girl. It goes back to a dumb resolve in college to stay clear of commercial radio. It goes back to my having a poor résumé and not getting hired by the AP or the Minneapolis *Tribune* where I could've been spectacularly miserable. It goes back to when I hired an illegal alien to take care of my apartment, a handsome black-haired Tibetan woman who saved her money and brought her daughters to America from Nepal and they all became legal and moved to California, and on the morning she said good-bye, she held both my hands in hers, and she cried harder than anyone I ever said good-bye to, and she left a long white silk Buddhist prayer scarf tied to the door handle, and ever since then, I've had so much good fortune, I can't tell you.

I was a pale awkward boy of no great acumen, drifting around on the periphery, and I managed to write myself into the center of things. I created a town and made myself the authority on it. I have been reckless, confused, sunk in misery, and squandered many chances. I have made sensible decisions that turned out to be stupendously dumb. But I go to work every day and I keep tearing off after the tennis ball on Saturday nights. Saturday is a 13-hour day and after *A Prairie Home Companion* I get in my car and drive up the hill to home. Change into jeans and a T-shirt, make a pot of mint tea, sit down and write my Sunday newspaper column. A good day. Not so bad a deal, though when I look out the window and see Nathan Hale in the dark, contemplating the gallows, I do think about my own dwindling life expectancy.

In July of 2001 I went down to the Mayo Clinic in Rochester and had an operation to sew up a leaky valve in my heart and by Labor Day I was on the road promoting a new novel. On September 10, 2001, I gave a reading at the Barnes & Noble bookstore on Union Square in New York City, and around midnight, I sat with a few friends at a sidewalk café on 14th Street, the World Trade Center towers shining in the night to the south of us, and enjoyed a big tray of Malpeque oysters and a Tanqueray martini. Eight hours later, it happened, the unthinkable, the black smoke and flame, the plane hitting the tower, the second plane banking into the second tower, the fireball, the buildings collapsing an hour later. I was up on West 90th Street and heard the first plane go over, heading down the Hudson at a desperately low altitude, and a few minutes later my phone rang and it was my friend Tony in the Village who had seen the fireball and was weeping. He said there were people leaping from the towers, like flowers falling, and then he could say no more.

It was, for a time, a catastrophe for which there was no name, there being no term for hijacking planes and crashing them into buildings, no single place name like Pearl Harbor, so people referred to it abstractly as It or "all of this," as in "Before all of this happened, we were thinking of going to Europe." Only after two or three months did people refer to it by its date, 9/11.

Like everyone else, I kept putting myself in the place of the people on the planes: you take off from Boston and ascend through the cloud cover and about the time you get out your laptop, there's commotion up front and sounds of struggle and men going through the cockpit door and panic wells up in your chest and you say the Lord's Prayer and something tells you that the end has come and you will never see your children again and the silly argument with your wife about the Visa bill was your last conversation.

Or you're standing in the dining room on the 101st floor, picking up coffee and a bagel and cream cheese and dreading the stupid conference about to begin, which you were hoping not to attend, and there is a jolt that knocks plates off the table, and you think, *Earthquake*, and then there is smoke, and you dash to the stairwell, and it's full of smoke, and you sit on the floor and call 911 on your cell phone, and something in the voice of the woman at the other end tells you: that's it, Bud, it's over. Those people on the 101st floor started their day out here on the streets with the rest of us.

All that week, we heard stories of men and women in the towers who, in a horrible moment, stifled their fear and tried to help other people. All week, New Yorkers went about their business quietly, thoughtfully—no horns honking, no cursing and flipping the bird, none of the usual smart-ass stuff—and on Friday, there was a twilight vigil all over the city. People stood on the sidewalk holding candles, in front of brownstones and luxury co-ops and public housing projects and on street corners, some of them singing "My Country 'Tis of Thee" and "America the Beautiful" and "Amazing Grace." I stood with a bunch on West 90th and then I walked around the Upper West Side and saw little groups of old lefties and die-hard liberals standing on sidewalks holding candles and singing about the fruited plains and spacious skies, the thoroughfare of freedom across the wilderness, and *O beautiful for patriot's dream that sees beyond the years; thine alabaster cities gleam undimm'd by human tears* and sang it with tears in their eyes in the midst of the shining city that was the dream of so many immigrant patriots. A little knot of singers in front of each building, New Yorkers in communion. Who organized this? Whose idea was it? I didn't know but at the moment it seemed almost spontaneous.

Soon after, the politicians moved in and the crass exploitation began, but the vigils were genuine.

Such a rare moment in New York and so fervent, the message one of simple communalism: we are all here together. Along with the pages and pages of obituaries in the *Times*, it was the most moving aspect of the week after 9/11—the spirit of New Yorkers silently rallying to each other. It reminded me of my first experience of New York, when Dad brought me to the city in August 1953. I was 11. He came to visit some friends in Brooklyn whom he'd met when he was stationed at the Army Post Office near Times Square during the war. We stayed with them in their little apartment in Brooklyn. One hot night, unable to sleep, Dad and I went for a walk and stopped at a candy store for a couple sodas and stood on the curb and drank them. Across the street was a park, a square really, a block long on each side, with trees and grass, park benches around the perimeter facing the sidewalk. The park was full of people sleeping on blankets. Families curled up together on the grass, asleep. Not hoboes: families, escaping from hot apartments to the cool outdoors, sleeping in a little island of dark in the middle of the great glittering city, and on the park benches sat men, smoking, talking in low voices, keeping watch over the sleepers. Dad and I stood and looked at them and nothing was said but that picture of nocturnal encampment became a permanent memory of the city, along with Ebbets Field, Coney Island, pushcart peddlers, the Empire State Building, and the Staten Island ferry. Utterly simple, completely astonishing.

September 2001 was the worst of times and the best of times. The event drove out trash TV for a week or so, and the lazy cynicism of the young, and talk radio started talking about something real. (There was a tone of maudlin self-absorption that crept in gradually, and on the first anniversary of 9/11 NPR broadcast two hours of claptrap, a couple dozen overwrought navel-gazers calling in to share their *feelings* about 9/11 and how it, like, meant for them, you know, like, the loss of innocence or something, people who had lost nobody in the disaster, hadn't been within a hundred miles of it, but nonetheless had *feelings* to share. It made you want to poison their fish tank.) Down in the Village, closed to motor vehicles, people walked in the streets, dust and smoke hung in the air but restaurants were open, even sidewalk cafés, people making heroic attempts at normal life, trying to enjoy a glass of wine and a bowl of steamed mussels and talk about movies and jobs and only mention in passing the horror and destruction a couple miles away. "Do you think they'll find survivors in the rubble?" "No, I doubt it." What a city. Hit with terrible force and two days later people were back at the movies. My New York friends Ellie and Ira and I had dinner at a steakhouse in NoHo that week, a quiet dinner at which we talked about everything but the disaster, and when I asked if they would go see the site, Ira looked at me and shook his head. Down near Trinity Church and Wall Street and the Woolworth Building, heartbreaking devastation, thousands of bodies, exhausted police and firemen, and all over the city, people in grief and shock, and yet classical musicians made the long trek down to St. Paul's Chapel a few hundred feet from the rubble of the towers and played Mozart and Bach and Haydn for the salvage workers taking a coffee break. Evil had struck us, but life went on and we accepted it as a gift. There is no closure, no resolution, we simply go on.

Who could have guessed in those quiet anguished days in New York the political rewards that the Republicans would reap from all those deaths? How George W.

Bush, having seen an intelligence memo in August warning that Al Qaeda was planning to hijack planes and fly them into tall buildings, which failed to engage his interest so he *didn't even call a staff meeting to discuss it*—after the horrors of 9/11 and the panic at the White House and the flight of Air Force One and Mr. Cheney taking control of the situation—Mr. Bush flew to New York and smartly stood amid the smoking rubble and spoke into a bullhorn and turned calamity into a photo op. Back in Washington, he snatched at a Democrat's idea for a security superagency and set out to create an immense new bureaucracy to paper over the mistakes of immense old bureaucracies and an ad agency came up with the weird name Homeland Security (*homeland*, a word Americans have never used to refer to the USA , a word you'd expect to hear spoken in a war movie by a man with a monocle flicking his riding crop against his shiny black boots), the Department of *Achtung*. Having failed in his duty, he wrapped the flag around himself and played patriotism like a $29 accordion and portrayed Democrats as Al Qaeda sympathizers and then launched a campaign of misinformation supporting a war against Iraq, which had exactly nothing to do with

9/11, exploiting the tragedy as the Defining Moment of his presidency, using it to squelch dissent and render the press supine and soften up the opposition to his right-wing judicial appointments and his gutting of the regulatory agencies, all of which would have been anathema to most of the people who died in the towers.

That was the stink drifting through the election of 2004. The New Yorkers and Jerseyites who died in the collapse of the towers and what this shallow and hard-shelled man failed to do for them that he had sworn to do and how he stood on their graves and gave a sermon diametrically opposite to what they believed—9/11 wasn't the "end of innocence," as some writers said, or a turning point in our history, it was a lapse of security exploited by the man who was purportedly in charge of national security at the time.

The men and women who rode the elevators up to work that morning came in on PATH trains from New Jersey or rode in on the Long Island Rail Road and then took the subway down to the WTC or they rode the Lexington Avenue subway down to City Hall and maybe walked across City Hall park behind the Boss Tweed building and the Woolworth tower. I used to have an office in the Woolworth. I remember the neighborhood. The crowds of suits heading to work, the bike messengers, the Wall Street crowd. There was a lunch wagon on the street with an Arab guy in it where I stopped for a cup of coffee and a bagel every morning, and after two mornings, he knew that I wanted a large coffee with milk and a poppy seed bagel with cream cheese and scallions. After two mornings he knew this. Now that's what you call free enterprise.

Those men and women were part of a world utterly different from that of George W. Bush's Texas. They belonged to a world of theater and books and street life and freedom of thought and the democracy of the subway. They deserved better than for their grave to become his platform.

I think of those New Yorkers hurrying along Park Place or getting off the No. 1 Broadway local, hustling toward their office on the 90th floor, the morning paper under their arms, and then I think of George W. Bush, and I feel a little heat behind the eyebrows.

But I refuse to be furious. I am a Democrat living in a great country, at home in St. Paul, Minnesota, where no matter what, there is a lot of satisfaction going on a good deal of the time. Complaint is a cherished art form, here as in New York, and we complain about the anger on the freeways and the teeth-grinders of AM radio and the gothic teenagers with chopped black hair and ugly tattoos and faces glittering with metal as if they'd fallen face-first into the tackle box. We complain about hoity-toity restaurants with attitudinous waiters serving half-ounce medallions of pork with an effusion of avocado on a white plate two and a half feet in diameter for $31, but in fact, life is pretty good. The streets of St. Paul are clean, the cops and firemen are the finest in the land, the parks are lovely, the old Victorian houses are cherished, and the new Italian restaurant three blocks from here, the one with the shady patio and the terrific risotto, is thriving. The social compact is still intact, knock on wood. Life is pretty good in St. Paul. Call it apathy, but really it's satisfaction. Or poise. As Whitman wrote:

> Me imperturbe, standing at ease in Nature,
> Master of all, or mistress of all—aplomb in the
>   midst of irrational things,
> Imbued as they—passive, receptive, silent as they,

Finding my occupation, poverty, notoriety, foibles,
   crimes, less important than I thought;
. . .
O to be self-balanced for contingencies!
O to confront night, storms, hunger, ridicule, acci-
   dents, rebuffs, as the trees and animals do.

When I was young I was more perturbed by irrational things and by rascals like Bush, I loved the insurrectionist aspect of politics, the forces of reason storming the Bastille, the good peasants baring their butts at the Blanc Palais, the king's courtiers mincing and fawning on *Meet the Press*, the royal artillery barrage of TV commercials, the ferocity of the peasants' attack on the royal flank, the shudder and screech as the regime collapsed in 1968 and again in 1974—it was all terribly gratifying back then in my salad days. I'm older now and mellower. Richard M. Nixon had his points: he went to China, he got the cleanup of the Great Lakes under way, he put Harry Blackmun on the Supreme Court. Lyndon B. Johnson was revealed in the transcripts of his long, anguished telephone calls to colleagues, a different

LBJ from the one we loved to despise back then; he was a man in despair over Vietnam who saw all too clearly the cataract he was being swept toward, that dreadful and wasteful war that poisoned our politics and slaughtered hundreds of thousands of people because Democrats were afraid of being called "weak on communism" and so the ship got on the reef and we didn't know how to reverse the engines.

You go to the Vietnam Memorial in Washington today and look at the names on the wall, you feel united with the folks around you, the families still in grief for boys long gone, the old vets, the schoolkids. All the political divisions that tore us up thirty years ago don't seem so important now compared to the loss of those lives. There is a feeling of solidarity that you also get at Gettysburg and Ellis Island and Valley Forge.

Someday the Vietnam War will mean no more to people than the War of 1812 and the wall will be something to lean against as you eat lunch and look at pretty girls and plan your weekend; I pray there will not be some new memorial to the dead of some new horror.

Most people treasure the sense of true national unity, which we briefly had after 9/11 until the Republicans took out a trademark on the tragedy—the sense of unity we try to relight every Memorial Day. (The Fourth of July is gone, a big dead hollow holiday, but Memorial Day retains a little of its spirit.) I feel that old American solidarity sometimes when listening to jazz, especially Armstrong and Ellington and Benny Goodman, the old guys who swept Europe and whose music was a living symbol to the Resistance of all that was worth dying for in the fight against Hitler. I feel it sometimes on my way out of the theater after a terrific performance of *Gypsy* or *The Music Man* or *Oklahoma!*—the American musical, a peculiar construction whose success depends on ensemble, not celebrity, and you sometimes see a student or amateur production that sweeps you away and it's exhilarating (to an American anyway), all those shining young faces, like seeing your kid's baseball team play over its head for nine solid innings, and all of us Americans walk out of the theater feeling unaccountably joyful together. I feel it sometimes at the ballpark, sometimes reading American poetry and seeing the heroism of poets, I feel it driving a car across Wyoming or through the Civil War battlefields of Virginia, Chancellorsville and the Wilderness and Fredericksburg and

Antietam, or along the Mississippi. I wish that Republicans had a little more genuine love of this country and weren't still hung up on the Sixties and so medieval in their worship of rank and hierarchy. They slid into Washington on an oil slick like a gang of small-time mafiosi and sold out representative democracy to their special patrons and backers and corrupted a lot of good Christian people in the process. This year, as in the past, they will portray us Democrats as embittered academics, desiccated Unitarians, whacked-out hippies and communards, people who talk to telephone poles, the party of the Deadheads. They will lie with astonishing enthusiasm and see lights in all the tunnels and denounce government as if they had not been in charge of things these many years. To which I say: "Good luck and good riddance."

We should establish reservations for angry Republicans and give them vast tracts of western North Dakota and Wyoming. Let them earn their living from the dry soil and be as paranoid and angry as they like. It's a big country.

Dante said that the hottest place in hell is reserved for those who in time of crisis remain neutral, so I have spoken my piece, and thank you, dear reader. It's a beautiful world, rain or shine, and there is more to life than winning. *The thing that has been is the thing that shall be; and the thing that is done is that which shall be done: there is nothing new under the sun.* And *the race is not to the swift nor the battle to the strong nor riches to men of understanding, but time and chance happeneth to them all.* Lord, have mercy.

As soon as I finish this book, I am going to walk around the block for a cup of coffee and watch the parade go by on Selby Avenue, sit at ease, passive, receptive, silent, in the midst of bad news, like a horse in a rain shower, like a bird on a branch, like the tree itself, cracked, one limb gone, and yet unperturbed. If you see me, come sit down, there is more to talk about.

FOR THE BEST IN PAPERBACKS, LOOK FOR THE

In every corner of the world, on every subject under the sun, Penguin represents quality and variety—the very best in publishing today.

For complete information about books available from Penguin—including Penguin Classics, Penguin Compass, and Puffins—and how to order them, write to us at the appropriate address below. Please note that for copyright reasons the selection of books varies from country to country.

In the United States: Please write to *Penguin Group (USA), P.O. Box 12289 Dept. B, Newark, New Jersey 07101-5289* or call 1-800-788-6262.

In the United Kingdom: Please write to *Dept. EP, Penguin Books Ltd, Bath Road, Harmondsworth, West Drayton, Middlesex UB7 0DA.*

In Canada: Please write to *Penguin Books Canada Ltd, 90 Eglinton Avenue East, Suite 700, Toronto, Ontario M4P 2Y3.*

In Australia: Please write to *Penguin Books Australia Ltd, P.O. Box 257, Ringwood, Victoria 3134.*

In New Zealand: Please write to *Penguin Books (NZ) Ltd, Private Bag 102902, North Shore Mail Centre, Auckland 10.*

In India: Please write to *Penguin Books India Pvt Ltd, 11 Panchsheel Shopping Centre, Panchsheel Park, New Delhi 110 017.*

In the Netherlands: Please write to *Penguin Books Netherlands bv, Postbus 3507, NL-1001 AH Amsterdam.*

In Germany: Please write to *Penguin Books Deutschland GmbH, Metzlerstrasse 26, 60594 Frankfurt am Main.*

In Spain: Please write to *Penguin Books S. A., Bravo Murillo 19, 1º B, 28015 Madrid.*

In Italy: Please write to *Penguin Italia s.r.l., Via Benedetto Croce 2, 20094 Corsico, Milano.*

In France: Please write to *Penguin France, Le Carré Wilson, 62 rue Benjamin Baillaud, 31500 Toulouse.*

In Japan: Please write to *Penguin Books Japan Ltd, Kaneko Building, 2-3-25 Koraku, Bunkyo-Ku, Tokyo 112.*

In South Africa: Please write to *Penguin Books South Africa (Pty) Ltd, Private Bag X14, Parkview, 2122 Johannesburg.*